BUDDHISM
AND
THE SCIENCE OF HAPPINESS

A personal exploration of Buddhism in today's world

by

William Woollard

Grosvenor House
Publishing Limited

This book is published by
Grosvenor House Publishing Ltd
28-30 High Street, Guildford, Surrey, GU1 3HY.
www.grosvenorhousepublishing.co.uk

A CIP record for this book
is available from the British Library

ISBN 978-1-907652-73-8

Dedicated to my beloved wife Sarah for her unfailing love and support

Acknowledgements

This book was born out of a series of talks I was invited to give in various parts of SGI-UK in 2009 and 2010. So warm was the response to those talks, which touched briefly on the idea of a science of happiness, that it gave me the inspiration and the confidence to explore further and dig deeper. And so with much reading and much burning of midnight oil, a handful of notes steadily grew into this book. So my thanks are due to Rose Fujii, for her gentle insistence that people would find such a theme interesting, to the many subsequent audiences who came to listen as the ideas grew in scope, and who asked such interesting questions, and to my new found friends overseas, Guy McCloskey of SGI-USA and Sergio Notari of SGI-Italy, who were kind enough to read the initial manuscript and offer a host of important suggestions.

A Note on the Author

Producer, director, writer, presenter, William's career covers the entire spectrum of television production. But he has experienced several other careers in an eventful life. Oxford graduate. A fighter pilot with the RAF. A trouble shooter for an oil company in the jungles of Borneo and the deserts of Oman. A social scientist working on corporate social responsibility with major international organisations in Europe and the USA. Finally an award-winning presenter and writer producing documentary programmes and writing scripts for some of the world's major networks.

Much travelled, twice married, four children. A life time interest in comparative religion and science among many other things. An earlier book on Buddhism, *The Reluctant Buddhist* has been translated into Italian and Spanish and Portuguese and now sells around the world.

Contents

Acknowledgements   v
A Note on the Author   vi

An Introduction
The Buddhist Perspective   ix

Chapter One
A Question of Our Time   1

Chapter Two
Who Are We?   21

Chapter Three
So What's Religion all About?   42

Chapter Four
What's so Special about Buddhism?   56

Chapter Five
Buddhism in the Modern World   74

Chapter Six
Buddhism Is Not A Morality   81

Chapter Seven
How to Strangle the Parrot   102

Chapter Eight
Buddhism and the Pursuit of Happiness   119

Chapter Nine
A Question of Attitude 129

Chapter Ten
A Brief Excursion into the Brain 141

Chapter Eleven
The Mystery of Mind 159

Chapter Twelve
Mind and Body 171

Chapter Thirteen
Changing the Wiring Diagram 179

Chapter Fourteen
A Kind of Revolution 193

Chapter Fifteeen
The Wealth Delusion 207

Chapter Sixteen
A Brave New World 220

Appendix A
Nichiren Buddhism in Today's World 227

Appendix B
The Practice 231

List of References 254

The Buddhist Perspective

There is a famous Buddhist text, always attributed to Shakyamuni himself, which goes,

'There is no path to happiness. Happiness is the path.'

It's a phrase that clearly has a wonderful resonance to it. But its key quality I think is that it enfolds such a profound completeness. It describes what might be called the perfect virtuous circle, complete in itself. If you seek to fathom its meaning, as a purely intellectual process, there is no way of breaking into it, to discover where the process starts and how it continues. You simply go round and round chasing your tail, or at least I do. I find that it's only when I release the intellect so to speak, and stand back, and measure this text against my own life, that it's meaning seems to become clearer.

But those are just words aren't they? What do they really mean, measure this text against my own life? It's not an easy process of thought but let me try to tease it out, because it lies right at the heart of what this book is about.

I have been practising Nichiren Buddhism for some 20 years now. Throughout that time, if I look back, I can honestly say that I have never actually pursued the idea of my personal happiness. Or at least I am not aware of having *consciously* framed my thoughts in that way. Obviously I haven't actively pursued non-happiness either! But basically if I look back over that time, I have just got on with living my life. The major change has been that I have tried hard to do that within the framework of my new-found Buddhist principles and values. So, very briefly, I have maintained a strong daily practice. That was very difficult at first, because I was continually questioning its value, but it has become much easier as the years have passed. I've tried to respond positively to all the situations that I have encountered in my life, good bad and indifferent. And when I've failed to respond as positively as I might have, I've tried to re-evaluate and get it right, or righter, next time around. Sometimes that's been easy, sometimes it's been extremely difficult, but I am aware of having made the effort, whether it was easy or difficult. And I think it's fair to say that I have worked hard at seeking to create value in the lives of people whom my life has touched, in the ways that have been available to me.

So what is the result of all that? Where have I ended up? The extraordinary thing is that I have ended up with the most powerful sense of well being and gratitude for all the things that are in my life. All of them. Buddhism has this wonderful word 'mindfulness,' and somehow, I'm not quite sure how, I have been able to develop a much greater sense of mindfulness. A greater awareness of, a greater gratitude for, the immense richness of my life, and the people in it, at every level from the briefest of encounters, to the deep and loving relationships within my innermost family. And I am aware of an ability to embrace everything that I encounter in my life. Not just the easy things. The good and the golden things. But the rough and the tough stuff as well. And there have been many tough things. As I write this for example I am involved in a battle against cancer that has gone on for many months and has involved me in a fair bit of physical and mental pain. But as soon as I became aware of the cancer's existence, so too I was aware of my ability to embrace it as part of me. And that came as something of a shock to me, that my deep sense of well being was not dependant on only good things happening in my life.

What I am saying is that this gradual transformation towards well being has occurred almost unconsciously, as I have gone about my ordinary daily life…as a Buddhist. And the implications of that statement seem to me to be inescapable. Put simply, it is saying that a Buddhist practice, if it is followed with some degree of care and commitment, has the potential to transform the unlikely and intractable stuff of daily life, ordinary, everyday, daily life, into a profound sense of happiness and well being and gratitude for the joy of living.

It is in that sense then, that I understand *with my life*, the meaning of that remarkable phrase, there is no path to happiness; happiness is the path.

An unexpected conjunction

Moreover, as I pull together some of the many disparate ideas and propositions that have contributed to the themes in this book, I find that they expose a surprising and quite unexpected conjunction. Namely that fundamental ideas about the nature of human motivation and behaviour that Buddhism has been teaching for centuries, find echoes, and embellishment, and amplification, in the kinds of findings that are coming out of modern social science. I choose those words with some care because it's crucial I think not to fall into the trap of using words like 'support' or still less, words like 'validation' in this context. That would be wholly inaccurate. The findings of modern social science don't *support or validate* Buddhist teachings. Not in any way. As far as I am aware there has never been a piece of research to validate a Buddhist teaching. These findings simply provide for us a set of new and quite different and profoundly illuminating perspectives.

In any case, as I have suggested on several occasions, the insights and perceptions about the nature of human life and motivation that have come down to us from the two and a half thousand years of the evolution of Buddhist thought, don't need anything resembling validation from modern science. They have proved their value many times over in the toughest laboratory there is…namely human life itself.

We can choose optimism as a way of life

This has turned out to be a very much more divergent journey than I ever intended when I set out, taking us into many more fields of science than I had anticipated, and some that might be thought to lie somewhat off the beaten track. Although with each of these issues, even if they have started out as seemingly peripheral, in each case they have had something special to contribute to the central quest, what do we *really* mean when we talk about the nature of human happiness? And it is unquestionably fascinating I think, that so many of the ideas and propositions coming out of psychological and neurological studies today, resemble so closely the kinds of ideas that Buddhism has been teaching for so long. Ideas that are by no means concerned with the margins of our life. They are, many of them profoundly life-changing, including this extraordinary idea that we can train our feelings to shape our lives in the way we choose. We are not trapped by the circumstances or indeed the state of mind that we find ourselves in now, or that we have lived through in the past. We can, that is, *choose* optimism and happiness as a way of life.

But even as I write that I am only too well aware of course that it is far easier to say than to achieve. As we all know only too well, few things are more difficult to change than deeply ingrained patterns of thought and behaviour. It has taken a lifetime to learn them and build them into our lives. You could say that they represent nothing less than who we are. So clearly it takes real energy and determination to set out to change them. We need the self-honesty to recognise that we want to change. We need the courage to put the change in motion. Above all perhaps we need the conviction that we have the potential to *achieve* the change, that we can genuinely move our lives forward.

And even then we can't do it without help. Without some sort of a discipline or structure around which we can reinforce the determination and build the change. That in essence is what a Buddhist practice offers us. It offers us a structure and a method that enables us to take hold of our lives in a rational and measured way, and move them in the direction we wish to travel.

Thus, despite the many stereotypes that prevail in the West, a Buddhist practice is not in any way esoteric or other worldly. It is immensely practical and down to earth. It has nothing to do with some reward or some paradise in an after life. It is wholly about a greater sense of well being amidst the often harsh realities of this one. So if you strip it down to its barest essentials, you might view it as a sort of personal, daily, life time training programme, aimed at showing us how to shift our whole lives towards the positive end of the spectrum, towards value creation. Not all that different in a sense, from a personal daily programme at the gym, aimed at achieving a higher level of physical fitness. Only with the Buddhist practice we are of course talking about spiritual muscle, and about developing a mental toughness and resilience.

What does that mean in terms of the ups and downs of daily life? Basically it means that instead of finding ourselves responding negatively or positively, to good or bad situations as they arise in our lives, now up now down, depending on the nature of the circumstances we encounter, we seek to build an inner core of optimism and resilience and confidence, so that we can more often respond positively, *no matter what* circumstances we encounter. Does that mean we banish anxiety from our lives? Of course not. We are only human. Doubts, anxieties, concerns, frustrations, all remain part of the daily mix, since they are all part of our essential humanity. But in my experience they don't take over, because we are learning all the time how to respond to them more positively and more creatively.

Out of nowhere comes hope

One of the statements that is often made about the practice of Nichiren Buddhism, and one that I recall most vividly from my early days of practice has to do with the emergence of hope. Basically it argues that when we are faced with a particularly difficult or immensely painful situation, and have absolutely no idea where to turn or how to confront it, when we start to chant about it, as if out of nowhere come hope.

Along with many others I have experienced that situation many times, not least, in my struggle with the implications of cancer these past few months. Of course the hope that arises isn't from nowhere, it comes from within, and it is the initial spark that is needed to unlock the situation, to quieten down the panic or the fear, and to ignite the process of recovery. More formal Buddhist texts sometimes use the word 'recognition' to describe this crucial process, the emerging sense we have that however impossible the situation may seem, a solution is possible, and that we can find *within ourselves,* the courage and the resilience to move towards it.

Of course, in no way can that be a one step operation, any more than we would expect a fitness programme to involve one visit to the gym! If we really seek greater fitness we all know that it involves genuine commitment to a sustained programme. In a similar way, if we really seek this durable optimism, it clearly involves commitment to learning how to grow it. We summon up from somewhere the determination to set out on the path of change, and the daily practice helps us to sustain it in our daily lives. And when we fail as we are bound to do, the practice provides the structure that enables us to pick ourselves up and get on with it again. And again. And again. And as we get on with it, Buddhism argues, it has very much the same effect as tossing a rock into a pond. As we change, and set about living our lives on the basis of a different set of principles, so the ripples spread out in ever widening circles.

We create our own environment

That is the fundamental promise, that as we change, we are steadily, imperceptibly perhaps, changing the environment we inhabit. As we change, as we move away from cynicism perhaps, or anger, or a basically self-focused approach to life with its concentration on our own ego, towards a more compassionate and more responsive approach to others, we find those same qualities reflected back at us from our environment. If we think about it for a moment, we can all accept that idea quite readily I think. We all know that there is a constant interplay between ourselves and the society or the environment immediately around us. If we cast around in our memories we can all recall some experience of that. We know that a profoundly negative or pessimistic view of life, even if it expressed in the life of just one person, can drag down the spirit of an entire group or organisation. Conversely, a determinedly positive and optimistic approach to life can be immensely influential and infectious even in the most challenging circumstances.

Many people would argue for example, that President Obama's powerful optimism, expressed in the memorable and repeated *'Yes we can'* phrase at the centre of his Commencement Address,[1] lifted the spirit of an entire nation. In many ways it echoed the spirit expressed by an earlier president, J.F. Kennedy in his Commencement Address some 50 years earlier, when he declared,

'Our problems are man made, therefore they can be solved by man, and man can be as big as he wants. No problem of human destiny is beyond human beings. Man's reason and spirit have often solved the seemingly unsolvable, and we believe we can do it again.'[2]

'*And man can be as big as he wants.*' Or, we might say, as positive and optimistic as he determines to be. Essentially Buddhism teaches no more, or indeed no less than that. What it adds, is the *method* by which we can grow our spirit so that we can embrace it and believe it.

So it argues, that when we set out on this purely *personal* journey towards greater optimism and resilience, towards greater happiness indeed, even though we may at the outset, be focused entirely on our own concerns, inevitably, with the Buddhist practice, it becomes a wider social impulse. It is if you like the stone that we personally are dropping into the global pool. And every stone, however small, however personal and intimate and seemingly insignificant it might be, creates ripples, and ripples create change. Our personal change may initially have an effect only upon a relatively close knit group, on family and friends and colleagues at work perhaps. But the effect is real, and as we carry on, as we sustain this movement towards a more positive approach to all the circumstances we encounter, so, Buddhism suggests, the ripples extend slowly, gradually perhaps, but nevertheless they continue, out into the local society and beyond.

In recent years psychologists have noted that what might be called the pivotal difference between happy and unhappy people is the presence or absence of rich and satisfying social relationships; the ability and the opportunity to share meaningful experiences with family and friends and colleagues and neighbours. Buddhism has been teaching that radical idea for many hundreds of years. Namely that we practice to enhance not simply our own lives, but the lives of those whom our life touches. Modern sociological research has come to recognise something very similar only in the past couple of decades. Even so that does represent a remarkable conjunction of views. And the extraordinary thing is that it seems to coincide with the beginnings of a seismic shift in the way society as a whole is prepared to evaluate the idea of progress, away from the strictly limited economic or financial measures that have dominated the 20th Century, towards some measure that embraces the idea of *individual well being.* That would indeed represent a wholly new beginning, a brave new world you might say. It is in essence, the goal to which this book is dedicated.

—∞—

CHAPTER ONE

A Question of Our Time

One of the many stereotypes that surrounds the general perception of Buddhism in the West is that it is very much about giving things up, or about introducing a kind of spare asceticism into our lives. The fact is that almost the reverse is true. Buddhism is focused on increasing our experience of the richness of our lives, and in the process it talks to us a great deal about happiness. Indeed it is alone among the major world religions in proposing the extraordinary idea that happiness in our daily lives isn't a matter of chance or accident, as we commonly believe, something that comes to us if we happen to be particularly lucky or fortunate, but essentially it is a matter of choice. Indeed Buddhism goes further, it argues that we can all, without exception, learn how to make that choice. The learning process involved it declares, is neither particularly difficult nor exclusive, nor is it dependent upon our circumstances. That is truly an astounding, life-changing idea, one that is clearly worth discussing at any time, since we're all keenly interested in the idea of happiness for ourselves and for those closest to us. But it is, I would suggest, an idea that is of particular relevance in the times that we happen to be living through. Why do I say that? Because, for the very first time in its history, science too, seems to have become keenly interested in the idea of happiness.

Happiness is of course a slippery and elusive sort of subject, precisely because it is so subjective. When we have a toothache we all know clearly what happiness is, it's the absence of toothache. But once the toothache has gone we revert to the imprecision. It may also be, I have come to believe, a somewhat lightweight word when it stands alone, for the range of feelings and emotions that it is being called upon to convey, and that we will undoubtedly encounter as we seek to unravel the arguments. But is it now quite as slippery as it once was? That in a sense has become a pivotal question, since never before in human history has there been so prolonged and so focused and so combined an effort, by the sociologists and the psychologists and the neuroscientists and others, to unravel for us the nature and the texture of this most desired and yet most elusive emotion. And they go further, they seek to explain to us just how we might come to benefit from a fuller and altogether deeper understanding of what it is that allows it to emerge in our lives.

In that sense it could be argued we live in very unusual times, in which very considerable and genuinely scientific energy, is focused on trying to gain a fuller understanding of emotions and qualities that are so basic to our humanity. The kinds of things that people have in their minds for example, when they profess to a sense of completeness or satisfaction with their lives, or having a stable and resilient and deep-seated sense of well being. The kinds of things you might say that are of the greatest value to all of us, since they enable individuals and societies to work more harmoniously and productively.

Some knowledgeable observers even suggest that we might be looking at the beginnings of a whole new science. Possibly. But at the very least we are being offered a whole new series of immensely valuable insights, a whole new way of looking at so many things about our motivations and our behaviour that we have until now taken pretty much for granted.

Exploring the nature and the extent of that offering, and the way in which it relates to the fundamental teachings of Buddhism, is essentially what this book is about. When I started out I hadn't envisaged that the journey would take us quite so far afield, into the worlds of the evolutionary biologist and the neuroscientist for example, as well as those of the sociologist and the religious philosopher, but with even a modicum of hindsight those diversions now seem inevitable. It turns out that only by embracing them, and drawing them into the heart of the discussion can we end up with a reasonably satisfying answer. What's more I like to think that even a brief exploration into those worlds brings untold benefits, since they turn out to be immensely exciting and illuminating places to visit in their own right.

Begin at the beginning

But let me back up a bit, and begin at the real beginning of this journey for me, where the idea for this exploration came from. Not so long ago, on a working trip overseas, I slipped into my bag a couple of very different books to occupy the slack time in between the meetings. One was the brilliant book by the theoretical physicist Brian Greene, entitled *The Elegant Universe* that basically takes us on a breathtaking journey through the history of physics from Newton to Einstein and on to modern string theory. I suppose I understood about half of it! The other was a collection of essays by one of today's greatest thinkers and writers on Buddhist philosophy, Daisaku Ikeda from Japan, on the writings of Nichiren Daishonin.

Nichiren Daishonin was a Buddhist priest who lived in Japan in the 13th Century. He basically spent his life interpreting and rendering more accessible to ordinary people the teachings of the first historically recorded Buddha, Shakyamuni. Nichiren is sometimes given the title, the Buddha for the Modern World. Why is that you might ask if he lived in 13th century Japan? It is at least in part because he was in many ways a modernist who thought well outside his own time. He evolved a daily practice, a method if you will, to enable ordinary people living in the real world and holding down a day job so to speak, bringing up a family and worrying about the mortgage or the tax bill, or caring for aged relatives and so on, to fold a strong, flexible and effective Buddhist practice into their lives and so to benefit from the profoundly life-changing principles and values inherent in Buddhism. That was Nichiren Daishonin's great legacy. It is a practice that has remained vibrant and alive and above all relevant down the intervening centuries. So much so that in the past few decades it has spread widely around the world, both east and west.

But back to Ikeda's essays themselves, they covered many themes, and one of the most important was the discussion of the power of compassion in our daily lives. Compassion in the broadest sense that is, not simply sympathy for or even empathy with, those in some difficulty, but essentially a deep sense of connectedness with everything we encounter in our lives, good bad and indifferent, so that we are better able to embrace it, or face up to it, and create the greatest value out of it.

4

Although I hadn't thought about these books in any particular way when I slipped them into my bag, as I went from one to the other during the trip, it became clear that in so many ways they represented almost perfect examples of the twin poles or the pillars around which swirls the current version of the debate that we loosely call science versus religion, the debate about the comparative roles of science and religion in our lives and in society. It is of course a discussion, an argument if you will, that has gone on for a very long time indeed. In some respects you could say it dates back even to classical times with the debate about the conflicting influence in our lives of Logos the god of reason and logic and Mythos the god of emotion and spiritual intuition.

But it has undoubtedly become markedly more heated and turbulent in recent times, as a number of eminent scientists have chosen to propound the view, in various articles and books, that basically science represents the only truth, that religion has passed it's sell-by date. That is not of course how they have put it, but I think it is fair to say that represents the essential argument. They have, more or less forcefully, expressed the view that religion, particularly divinely based religion, is a snare and a delusion, and has little useful contribution to make to modern life since we now have science to answer all our fundamental questions about the nature of life.

A crucially important debate.

So this is clearly not a marginal issue is it? It lies slap bang in the centre of our lives. We live at a time that is undoubtedly dominated by the processes of science and technology, and the idea that only scientific explanations are *rational* ones has become implicit in a great deal of western thought. It is

5

undoubtedly true of course that science is more than ever changing our lives, and we certainly need in some measure, to be engaged with scientific developments. But I would suggest that the pendulum has swung way beyond that balance point. In fact we've reached a situation where in virtually any public debate, scientific truth easily out trumps religious or spiritual truth, and we have come more or less to take that for granted. But is that an appropriate reflection of how we live and think about our lives?

My own view is that this is a crucial starting point on this journey towards a better understanding of what happiness is all about, because it governs so much that is fundamental to how we think about our lives and the way in which our societies work. Science and religion I suggest, far from being in conflict, should be seen as two deeply complementary ways of reaching an understanding of reality.

So where to start? Let me begin by giving two brief tasters from the two books I have mentioned, that clearly illustrate the two very different views of reality that science and religion can present us with.

Different versions of reality

So in the Brian Greene book for example there is a wonderful passage where he argues that 'it is wondrous…' that's the phrase he uses…it is wondrous, that over the space of just a few hundred years, human beings living on a pint-sized planet, orbiting a run-of-the-mill, star, out on the edges of a relatively undistinguished galaxy, have been able simply by observation and analysis, to work out the entire structure of matter right across the vastness of the known universe, from the giant super galaxies orbiting out there on the edge of darkness, down to the smallest particles that make up everything we know and see and touch, including ourselves. It's wondrous he says and he's right isn't he? It is an extraordinary feat of the human intellect, and it represents precisely the immense contribution that science makes to all our lives.[1]

Then in the Ikeda essays,[2] there is a brief passage where he talks of the fact that although we have the knowledge and the technology to be able to plant a man on a precise spot on the surface of the Moon, nonetheless that science doesn't help us one iota, in seeking to assuage the grief, the bottomless grief, of a mother whose beloved 16 year old son has just died. That is so simply put, but it strikes like a rapier to the very heart of the matter. He is writing about a real incident, a mother who lived in 13th Century Japan whose son died suddenly of a brief illness, one of Nichiren Daishonin's followers in fact. But the sentiment will strike just as keenly to the heart of a mother who has just lost her teenage son to a street stabbing in Hackney, or in Queen's, or in Mumbai. Indeed it strikes just as keenly to my heart, I have a wonderful sixteen year old son.

We clearly need both

But the key point I would want to make is that if we wish to live lives that we can truly grasp and inhabit and understand the meaning of, we clearly need both of these perspectives all the time, don't we? Both these kinds of illumination. We need the external illumination if I may put it that way, that comes from science, that paints for us as no other sphere of human activity can, the vast panoply of the universe within which we live out our lives. And we need the internal illumination that comes to us from religion, that speaks to us as no other sphere of human activity can, of our joys and griefs and moments of inner darkness. Inner darkness in our lives is real of course. It's as real as rocks. It's just made of different stuff.

So these spheres of activity are clearly different. No question. They occupy quite different, albeit overlapping dimensions in our lives. But I would argue that it is difficult to see the rational justification, or more importantly, the *value* to our lives, for viewing them as being in conflict, or that one should feel the need to drive out the other. That suggests it seems to me, more a rigidity of thought and a profound failure of the imagination, than the outcome of reasonable argument.

The scientific delusion

Nowhere perhaps is this idea expressed more powerfully, the rationality and therefore the validity of science, as opposed to the supposed irrationality and therefore the invalidity of religion, than in books such as Richard Dawkins' *The God Delusion.*

Dawkins is undoubtedly a brilliant writer and perhaps the most powerful advocate of the icily reductionist scientific position. So much so that although his primary target in this book happens to be the divinely based religions, when he argues that religion is not simply irrational, but the very enemy of rationality, and as such must be resisted and overcome since it leads people astray, inevitably all religions are in some measure caught and tainted by the argument.

In response one has to say that this point of view does lead him into some positions that seem difficult to sustain. He is compelled to argue for example, that some religions that have a heritage that goes back many thousands of years, and that have many millions of profoundly committed followers in the world today, aren't *really* religions at all, whatever their followers believe. And in a similar vein he is led to argue that Einstein's frequently expressed religious views, which were clearly central to Einstein's view of life, and the role of science in that life, and much else besides, weren't *really* religious at all, whatever Einstein himself may have thought. This is a difficult argument to accept, given that it suggests that Einstein simply didn't know what he meant by religion, when he famously wrote, '*Science without religion is lame, and religion without science is blind.*'

And Dawkins goes further, to argue essentially that the many scientists who genuinely express religious views, cannot really mean what they say. As scientists they must be atheists he argues.[3]

But science clearly has limitations

As you might expect, there are many in the scientific community who would take issue with these views, and it's important I think to hear some of those voices to redress the balance. Stephen Jay Gould for example, the American palaeontologist and outstanding science writer coined the definitive acronym to help us navigate through this difficult area. The acronym is NOMA. It stands for non overlapping magisteria, which is simply a high flown academic way of saying that science basically doesn't *do* religion, it doesn't have the tools or the methods to cope with this immense spiritual and emotional dimension of our lives. It's not really in a position that is to say, to express a view.

Dr. Richard Sloan, Professor of Behavioural Medicine at Columbia University covers the same sort of territory when he writes;

'Religion and science address different concerns…the concern I have is that science operates in a reductionist way, and if you try to understand the spiritual experience or a religious experience from the science perspective, ultimately you are going to reduce it to the coursing of neurochemicals in the brain. And while that may be satisfying to the scientist, it is anathema to the theologian, which illustrates the limits of science. There are some questions for which science cannot provide an adequate answer.' [4]

Indeed there are. Professor Martin Rees, cosmologist and President of the Royal Society in the UK, says something very similar when he argues that questions about why anything exists lie beyond the remit of science; science is essentially about the what and the how he argues. It's Religion that seeks to deal with the why.

The great American linguist and philosopher Noam Chomsky expresses a typically oblique view in his landmark book *Language and the Problems of Knowledge* when he writes;

'It is quite possible…overwhelmingly probable one might guess…that we will always learn more about human life and human personality from novels rather than from scientific psychology. The science-forming capacity is only one facet of our mental endowment. We use it where we can but are not restricted to it, fortunately.' [5]

Perhaps the most important word in that passage is the closing one, the immensely potent *'fortunately.'*

And last but by no means least, Lawrence Krauss, physicist and astronomer and science writer from Case Western Reserve University in Ohio speaking at a scientific seminar in La Jolla California,

'Science's success does not mean it encompasses the entirety of human intellectual experience.'[6]

That is the fundamental point isn't it? The absolute key to the argument. The entirety of human experience is the issue here, the full breadth and depth and passion of our essential humanity. No one questions the obvious truth that the advances in science and technology have brought immeasurable benefits to all our lives. We cannot conceive of civilised life without them. But the great fallacy, delusion even, that seems to me to lie at the heart of *The God Delusion,* and one that has been noted by several reviewers, philosopher and writer Mary Midgley among them, is that Dawkins seems to assume that science is the *only* valid source of knowledge. Whereas the plain fact is that science is only a relatively small and highly specialised part of what we all know.[7]

We learn about life from life itself

Most of our knowledge it is clear, comes from our own experience of life. What has been described by the psychologists as 'tacit knowledge.' And if you think about it even briefly, that is the only way that we could get on with all the tumultuous ebb and flow of our daily lives. In no way could it be a process of establishing hypotheses and testing them out. As a result of our experiences we are constantly making and updating and re-updating assumptions about ourselves and other people and the world about us. It's a constant flow of experience and assumption, far too general and far too rapid and informal ever to be fully tested out. We all learn about life you might say from the flow of life itself. Even the most hardened scientists among us.

And when it comes to answering those big, bottomless questions we mentioned earlier, such as why are we here, or is there a purpose and meaning to life, we don't turn to science do we? How could we since it has nothing to say on these issues? We turn to a much less formalised and in many ways more emotional area of our lives, which we happen to have labelled as religion. There is much about our lives that is indeed mysterious. As we all know, self-knowledge can be a lifetime's work. It takes that long to understand even a fraction of who we really are, and we are constantly being surprised and taken unawares by the swiftly shifting currents of our own emotions and responses, let alone other people's.

The key questions about life

So science undoubtedly derives its power and its persuasiveness from the fact that its assertions can be checked and re-checked against the real world we inhabit. That's how science works. Which means we are perfectly entitled to ask of science the ultimate question, Is it right? Is it true? Because that is the nature of the claims that scientists make for their findings. They claim to reveal a new piece of truth about the universe. Although of course as the philosopher Karl Popper reminds us, it is fundamental to scientific advance that the current 'truth' might well be superseded sooner or later by a different version of the truth.

But those scientific assertions can cover only a relatively small fraction of the vast totality of human understanding and experience. We can't for example put the issues that religion is primarily concerned with, such as love and anger or compassion and courage into a test tube and weigh and measure them. We are therefore entitled, required even, to ask of religion a quite different question, which is basically, does it work? Does it help us to live more value creating lives? Does it lead to a greater sense of stability and well being in our lives? Does it sustain us when the going gets tough? Does it above all, help us to develop our compassion, which is probably the most important human quality of them all, living as we now do on such a crowded planet?

A simple street-level example

It might help to give one simple current example of the fundamental distinction I am trying to make. At the moment scientists, particularly physical scientists, are bedazzled by the colossal, cathedral-like, Large Hadron Collider in Geneva, probably the largest and most expensive scientific instrument ever seen on the face of the planet, because they believe it will tell them something new about the nature of matter. And all that is immensely exciting of course. Exactly what science is all about.

But science is not the slightest bit interested in how I personally manage to generate and sustain the compassion that enables me to have a caring and meaningful relationship… with a somewhat cantankerous neighbour. Whereas religion, in my case Buddhism, is of course deeply interested in such a small and personal issue, and what's more, it's prepared to go to considerable lengths to teach me just how I may generate that compassion, and use it in this and all the other areas of my life.

It is as I've said, a simple even trivial example, but the plain fact is that the nature of matter…and indeed the nature of cantankerous neighbours… are both genuine parts of our reality, and the one is no more important than the other.

All that really goes to show that science and religion clearly address different issues and have quite different ways of thinking about reality, but both clearly have a role to play if we are seeking the fullest experience of life. It seems self evident that we need the understanding and the illumination that comes from both science and religion, if we are to build the richest and most meaningful and creative lives of which we are capable. They are deeply complementary. I rest my case.

A new era

But it was really as a result of that process of argument, and the fact that over recent years an increasing number of social scientists have become deeply interested in this area of human motivation and behaviour, that it occurred to me that in a sense, we are living through a wholly new era, and one in which a wholly new overlapping of interests has developed.

Buddhism offers a fundamental proposition to all of us, namely that the purpose of life is the *attainment of happiness*, the building of a sense of confidence and optimism and well being, that is strong enough and resilient enough not to be dismantled by the challenges and the difficulties we are all bound to encounter in our lives, whatever our circumstances. It has now become possible, essentially for the very first time, to take that life-changing proposition and to look at it both from the classical Buddhist perspective, and equally from the scientific perspective, to see whether those fundamentally different approaches bring us any new insights or understanding. That represents it seems to me, an extraordinary opportunity that should not be let slip.

Buddhism is unlike all other major global religions in that it is not attached to any definition of divinity. Shakyamuni Buddha, the first historically recorded Buddha, and the seed from which this immense tree has grown, was an ordinary human being. Immensely wise and perceptive and charismatic no doubt, but at no time in his long and passionate teaching career did he claim to have a divine connection, a hot line to God so to speak. This clearly differentiates him from the other great founders of religions such as Jesus and Mohammed, who claimed throughout their lives to be driven by divine inspiration, the messengers on earth of the divine will.

This clearly gives Buddhism a very special quality indeed. By definition it cannot be about so many things that we take for granted as being part and parcel of the nature of formalised religion, such as obedience to an external god-given code of behaviour or morality, or the centrality of divine praise and thanksgiving. There is no place for any of that or indeed anything close to it.

The fundamental objective

Thus with its essential humanism, its belief in the power and resilience of the individual human spirit, Buddhism is strongly focused on the pursuit of happiness as *the* fundamental objective of human life. That is life in the here and now, rather than in some heavenly hereafter, which is of course a key differentiator. In that sense it seeks to harness what is undoubtedly one of the most powerful motivators in human life as an engine of change, to enable us to learn how to live fuller and happier lives in the very midst of life's problems and challenges. It teaches that achieving happiness for ourselves *and others*...that is a primary qualification, it cannot be our happiness *at the expense* of or *in disregard of* others... is essentially what life is about. But as you would expect, happiness isn't waiting to be plucked off a tree like a piece of ripe fruit. Wanting it isn't having it. We have to *learn* how to achieve it or how to *create* it for ourselves. We have to take that is, the lumpy and discordant and disturbing material out of which all our daily lives are fashioned, and learn how to *transform* it into the stuff of happiness.

So happiness in Buddhism is unquestionably not defined, as it so often is in the dreams we create for ourselves, as the *absence* of problems for example. Of arriving at some place or some space in our lives, where everything is sunshine and blue skies. That clearly is the stuff of dreams, whereas Buddhism is daily life. Thus happiness in Buddhism is defined very much in terms of learning the kinds of *attitudes and values we need to master*, to enable us to build this sense of confidence and stability and optimism that is strong enough and resilient enough not to be blown away by all the tough stuff we encounter, by the problems and the setbacks and the sorrows, that we all struggle with on a daily basis.

That in essence, is the promise that comes with a Buddhist practice.

Two basic questions

So in all that follows we are really seeking an answer to two utterly basic questions, questions that anyone approaching a Buddhist practice would I suggest, really want to have the answers to. Does that fundamental Buddhist proposition stand up? Does it make sense in terms of the way we live and experience our daily life? And second, does the kind of observation and analysis that is now being applied to this area of human life by the social scientists and the psychologists, (looking at happiness and well being and confidence and resolution), have anything to add to our understanding of what is involved in trying to achieve it?

That having been said, it's important I think, to underline what is a crucial point. Namely, that the insights and perceptions on the nature of human motivation and behaviour, that have come to us from some two and a half thousand years of evolution and development in Buddhist thinking, don't need the *validation* or the *justification* of science. Not in any way. They stand very much on their own, as the insights and perceptions of some of the greatest minds in human history. So we need to be clear that it's not *validation* we are seeking here. It is solely the *understanding* that comes from a different perspective, or the revealing new insights that the new knowledge coming out of the studies and research programmes might bring.

A change of perspective

Because it's clear that there is a great deal at stake here for all of us. If these perspectives help clarify for us in any way, the kinds of things that *do* bring a sense of completeness and confidence and resilience into people's lives, and, just as important, the things that *do not*, then they clearly have the potential to be life changing.

And I ought to add perhaps, that as I write those words, they do take me back sharply to the beginnings of my own Buddhist practice. I was for a long time deeply sceptical about the relevance or appropriateness of a Buddhist practice, not just to my life, although of course that was the core of the issue, but to a western way of life in general. Immensely competitive as it is, immensely achievement driven, immensely materialist in many of its motivations. Motivations that I share in large measure. They are part of my life. When I described myself in those days as being a *reluctant* Buddhist,[8] it was very accurate. But if I try to think myself back into that situation, it's clear that there was resolution there too. I was determined that once I had set out on this somewhat unexpected path, I would continue until I was sure, one way or the other, about the effect of a Buddhist practice in my life. It was easy enough for people to say to me, '*Buddhism is daily life.*' The question was, did it actually work at that level? Did it make a real difference to the way I responded to people and situations in my workaday everyday life?

In my reading, and in my conversations with practising Buddhists I had gained a glimpse that it might well do that. When I went to Buddhist meetings for example, there was a genuine sense of …well of optimism and confidence, even when people were talking about all kinds of difficulties and challenges. Life for these people was clearly about seeing the problems for what they were, challenging them, and trying to see them not simply as a problem, but actually as opportunities for change. That was the key thing, *seeing* them differently. Ordinary people with ordinary everyday problems, learning to see things differently through the focusing lens of their practice. Sometimes succeeding. And sometimes failing of course, but having the courage and the resilience to pick themselves up and press on. That is easy to say of course. Setting it down in a few short lines like that, it scarcely creates a ripple. It's only when we have to do it that we realise just how much courage and resilience it takes.

But if I squeeze all that into a nutshell, I would argue that therein lies the true greatness of a Buddhist practice. It really lies in that simple, un-dramatic process, trying to achieve that slight shift in perspective. And strange as it may seem, that is all that is needed. It may only be a slight change, but time and time again it proves to be enough to enable us to tackle the problem with a completely different, more optimistic attitude, that then leads on to a tangible, positive, sometimes even dramatic change in someone's life. And every time it does so, it strengthens the resolve to deal with the next issue that comes along in the same way. We find it possible to move from being generally anxious and negative about problems, and cast down by them, to being focused and positive and even confident that we can find a way through them.

And there is no question that in the increasing pace and turbulence and complexity of modern life, that is an immensely valuable skill to acquire.

Holding a mirror up to Buddhism

And if we now move from the Buddhist perspective, and look at many of the findings that have emerged in recent years from the scientific one, the research that has been carried out in this field on the kinds of values and behaviour that generate a profound sense of well being in people's lives, it is extraordinary how closely they mirror so many of the lessons that have been embodied for so long in Buddhist teachings. And there is nothing out-of-the-way or exotic about these lessons. They are all very ordinary, everyday kinds of behaviour, well within the compass of ordinary lives. Buddhism we are reminded constantly, is nothing more nor indeed less, than daily life.

So altruism and compassion for example come very high on the scientific list, giving rather than taking, concerning oneself with the needs and welfare of others, rather than focusing solely on one's own current crop of problems. Evolutionary biologists still struggle over working out the *evolutionary* value of altruism, and yet here it is, revealed as a powerful and primary source of human happiness. The remarkable power of gratitude is a recurring theme, unlocking, as the researchers put it, a whole cascade of benefits both for the giver and the receiver, and anybody within earshot. Gratitude is very good news for the spirit.

Other key factors that emerge from the research are the huge importance of a sense of self worth, and of having some goal or objective that is bigger and wider than the simple daily progression of our lives. They even talk, in wholly un-mystical language it must be said, about the value of learning how to live in the *now,* in the experience that we are having at this moment, rather than being, as is so often the case, mired in the past or anxious about the future And perhaps above all the scientists talk of a sense of what they choose to call *engagement.* Essentially a strong sense of connectedness or involvement with the lives of those around us, friends and neighbours and work colleagues, since it refreshes and re-invigorates our sense of our wider humanity and our connection to other lives. We are in our deepest nature, gregarious animals.

So where does that leave us as we set out on this journey down the yellow brick road, towards understanding rather more keenly, what we mean when we use this slippery word… happiness? This chapter was by way of being an introduction to many of the themes we deal with in rather more detail as we travel. But it does also I hope, reinforce the validity of the basic approach. Buddhism has been talking about happiness to those prepared to listen, for a very long time indeed. Science has only been talking about it for a couple of decades. There is much to learn from both.

But we start out by asking who we really are?

—m—

CHAPTER TWO

Who Are We?

That might seem a somewhat strange question to pose at the beginning of a journey which seeks to bring a deeper understanding of our self. Because that of course is the essence of a quest for a greater sense of well being and of happiness in our lives, that's what it's all about. Psychologists and evolutionary biologists not to mention Buddhists, describe that quest for happiness as the ultimate motivation, in the sense that it requires no further description or definition. It is if you like complete in itself. If you ask yourself the blunt question what it is above all that you seek for your own life, and your partner, and children, and friends and colleagues, the answer comes out as happiness, a happy and fulfilled life. Every time. The obverse of that, a sort of generalised dissatisfaction with our lives or a low level background anxiety, or feeling out of kilter or out of balance with ourselves, all of which as we know are very widespread in modern society, come not just from a lack of self knowledge, but a general lack of understanding about how to go about achieving the well being bit. How to head out in the right direction so to speak. The American Psychologist Daniel Goleman[1] has dubbed our times as *'The age of melancholy,'*[1] because there is more depression about than in previous generations.

We also live in the age of the quick fix, and there are lots of them about. Personally I don't know of any rapid-fire routes to a solid and unshakeable sense of well-being at the core of one's life. Human behaviour is indeed malleable, that is one of our greatest strengths, for which we should constantly give thanks. But in my experience it takes commitment and determination and knowledge, real self- knowledge. We have to understand who we are, and the resources that we can call upon from within, to enable us to achieve what we earnestly seek.

Hence this somewhat oblique entry. If we are seeking to build a base that is solid and unshakeable then, I am suggesting, there is a virtue in the first building block being about our roots. Our deepest roots. Where did we come from? What were our nearest ancestors like? Being in a position to ask those questions is, if you think about it, a uniquely human privilege. This ability to explore our evolution, together with our ability to explore our consciousness, is what separates us from the rest of the animal kingdom. And to be honest I have to admit to a personal bias; I am utterly hooked on the narrative of our recent evolution, although I've tried to restrain that personal bias by telling it as briefly as I can, and still make sense.

It's a story that starts, in a deep cave in southern France.

The discovery

Montignac is a small village in South Western France in the valley of the Vezere River. It is limestone country, part of the Massif Centrale that dominates the topography of this part of France, and a region that is famous for its deeply cut river gorges, and the many caves and tunnels that have been carved over the centuries into its hillsides and valleys. On a warm September afternoon in 1940 four young men set out from the village and climbed into the nearby woods. They carried ropes with them and makeshift lamps because they were bent on exploration. A few days earlier one of them had come across a deep hole in the ground that seemed to have been exposed by a fallen tree. When they reached the hole it didn't take them long to widen the entrance. At first they dropped down some rocks to test its depth, then they fastened the ropes around a nearby tree and squeezed through the entrance into the darkness beyond. The hole was steep and slick with mud and clay, and they half fell, half slithered down into the blackness until they came to rest on what seemed to be a level surface of rock.

The leader struck a match and lit his oil lamp and held it up above his head to light up the cave around them. What met his gaze was astonishing to these young men, something that was completely beyond their experience or their understanding. Seeking to understand it and explain what they saw has since played a major role in re-writing the course of human pre-history, and in our new-found understanding of the people who became us, modern man.

The surface of the rock before them was covered with brilliantly painted animals. Bison, and galloping horses and aurochs and wild cattle. All painted with a passion and an energy and so keen an eye for the essential vitality and the spirit of these animals that to see them for oneself even today, is to take the breathe away, with their flowing manes and flying hoofs and savage horns and knowing eyes.

Where had they come from these paintings? What kind of people had this level of artistic ability, to use form and colour to create not just a two dimensional representation of the animals that roamed the woods and valleys around them, but a profound re-creation of the emotional impact they must have had upon the hunter, when he witnessed them afar off fleeing at the beginning of the chase, or close to as the hunt came towards its end? You get the distinct impression that the hunter or the painter, whichever it was, actually loved these animals that were so much part of his life, and more, he understood their character. Why had there been no precursors of this level of artistic skill? No slow fumbling steps of experiment with shapes and colours.

And why had they painted them so deep into the caves? Not, as you might expect, in the cave mouths or entrances where there was more light, and where the hunters might have taken shelter during a winter storm, or as the night drew in. The walls that were painted were deep within the dark and inaccessible bowels of the cave. The painter or painters must have needed the light of primitive oil lamps to see to do their work. Often they must have used some kind of scaffolding to reach so high on the walls. And to gaze in wonder at them, or perhaps to take part in the bonding rituals to which they bore witness, the members of the family or the tribal group for whom they had been painted, would have to be led and guided and squeezed through narrow passages and tunnels, often for several miles into the echoing depths of the darkness. They are frightening these caves, in their darkness.

It may seem strange, at first blush, to begin this attempt to unravel the nature of the unending human quest for a full and fulfilling and happy life… in the depths of a cave in the Dordogne. But that in a sense is where the story starts.

Where all our individual stories start. Because these cave paintings and the extraordinary culture of which they were a part, is an intimate part of the heritage that led to who we are and where we are now.

Our direct ancestors

The answers to the questions these cave paintings pose, tell us much about these people, who lived in Europe only some 40,000 years ago, and they tell us much about ourselves, because these people were our direct ancestors. The ancestors of you and me, and Shakyamuni and Socrates and Shakespeare and Mozart and Ghandi and Barrack Obama. They had the same brain, the same tall, light- boned body, the same straight-up forehead and flat cheek bones. They are us, in a way and to an extent that no previous ancestors were. Indeed to paraphrase one modern anthropologist, if you were to give them a good shave and a haircut and put them in a well-cut Pierre Cardin suit, then they could travel on the underground to Canary Wharf or to Grand Central Station without turning a head. Just as the art that they produced with such a powerful emotional and symbolic content, has the power to stir our hearts today, as it must have stirred theirs all those years ago.

They share with us the same Latin tag, *Homo sapiens sapiens*, or doubly wise man, to indicate the sheer scale of the gap that separates our hugely powerful brain and our behaviour from that of all other animals, including all the earlier hominids, that sit on the lower branches of the family tree. What is undoubtedly remarkable is that in the years since those young men made their extraordinary discovery at Merignac, now known around the world as the Lascaux Caves, a wholly different story has begun to emerge of who we are and where we came from.

As the anthropologist and writer James Shreeve has expressed it,

'The fact is human beings…modern humans, Homo sapiens sapiens, are behaviourally far, far away from being 'just another animal.' The mystery is where and how and why the change took place. There are no answers to be found in the vast bulk of hominid time on the planet. An all- important transition did occur, but it happened so close to the present moment that we are still reeling from it. Somewhere in the vestibule of history, just before we started keeping records on ourselves, something happened that turned a passably precocious animal… into a human being.'[2]

The evidence of that 'all important transition' and its extraordinary closeness to our present time is abundant. Many more sets of cave paintings similar to those at Lascaux have been discovered in Southern France and Spain. They were painted by quite different hunters or artists, separated by hundreds of miles of terrain, and by several hundred years of habitation, but they share a common spirit, a common vitality and exuberance and artistic ambition. Not just horses, but madly galloping and leaping and mane-tossing horses, and charging bulls and ibex clashing horns, and stags bellowing their mating call, and wild cows with great bellies heavy with their unborn calves. There is little if any representation of the artist men or women themselves, although in several cases the artists offer an enigmatic signature, a palm print, five fingers of the hand that has just displayed its skill. Nor have there been any findings of what you might call 'trainee' sites, where would-be artists might have tried out their hand so to speak, to seek the line that best displayed the aggressive thrust of the bison's horns or the wild flow of the horse's mane.

A new kind of mind

This astonishingly accurate and emotion-laden art seems to have come fully formed. And it wasn't alone. With it, in the same span of time, came what has been called a 'creative explosion' in a host of other technologies. Where before there had passed many tens of thousands of years, during which virtually no movement or progress had been made in the design for example of primitive stone tools and weapons, suddenly the archaeological sites in France and Spain and the Central European Plains and elsewhere are filled with exciting new artefacts. It was as if a new kind of mind, a new kind of imagination was at work. There was a whole new passion about the shape and the look and the feel of things. A wholly new concern for experimentation and innovation, new shapes, new designs, new materials, new complexities.

The archaeological sites begin to reveal not just new types of stone tools made in completely different styles and with different technologies, but a whole series of stylish and beautifully finished and decorated implements carved from antlers and animal bones and ivory. There were the beginnings almost of a modern-seeming life style, evidenced by items such as sewing needles and barbed spear points and fish hooks and ropes. There were even stone oil lamps, which could bring light into darkness, and vastly more effective cooking hearths, where the temperature could be controlled by the way the stones were placed. And where there were no natural caves in the hills, there are places where these early modern humans had begun to build quite complex clusters of huts.

The great question that is posed by this sudden flowering of imagination and inventiveness is when? When did mankind become modern? When did he acquire this sharp, divergent, flexible brain that led him in so many different directions so swiftly. In the past half century, since the discovery of cave paintings and fish hooks and carved harpoons and beautifully decorated and personalised spear throwers, several theories have been put forward by the archaeologists and the anthropologists in an attempt to give closer definition to this sudden flowering of modern skills and technologies.

As you might expect the debate and the controversy continue, but only to an extent. It's fair to say that one extraordinary hypothesis has become dominant in the field. First put forward some 15-20 years ago, it is now buoyed up by a growing body of fossil evidence from the archaeological digs around the world, and above all by the latest cutting-edge DNA evidence from the laboratories. But it is a theory that is so unexpected, so startling in its implications, that for most of us I'm sure, it completely re-shapes the casual view we have formed of our origins at school say, and in our diverse reading since.

Walking out of Africa

Most of us will have some memory of the human or hominid time line, often illustrated in the text books with drawings of little people, walking across the page from left to right, slowly becoming less hairy, and taller and more upright, and leading pretty close to the right hand edge of the page, to the man we call homo erectus, upright man. The fossil record suggests that although he was undoubtedly upright in posture, he was still substantially shorter than us, with a brain perhaps little more than half the size of ours, but his great claim to a pre-eminence in our time line, was that he was the first man to walk out of Africa. He did so perhaps a million years ago, driven northwards out of East Africa it seems by climate change and increasing desertification. He walked across the narrow hinge of land that joins Africa with Asia along the eastern rim of the Mediterranean basin, where Israel sits today. And from there, over many tens of thousands of years, he spread slowly northwards and eastwards until he had colonised much of the known world. In different parts of the world his characteristic fossil remains have been given different local names, Peking Man for example and Java Man. And the long- held conventional view has been that modern man, the people we are today, in our various ethnic groups, has evolved in these various parts of the world in an unbroken line from this original and ancient diaspora.

What is so startling is that the dominant modern thesis utterly re-writes that story.

It argues that there was in effect a second, and decisive walking out of Africa that occurred only about 90 to 100,000 years ago. Only the day before yesterday if we are talking in evolutionary time scales. Modern man, this tall, long-legged, light-boned, large-brained modern man, our direct ancestor, Homo sapiens sapiens, again driven by climate change, also walked across the narrow Palestinian bridge. The traces of his passage and his temporary residence have been found in abundance, in the caves in the hills behind Tel Aviv and Haifa.

The first signs of his arrival in Europe appear about 40,000 years ago, roughly the date of those cave paintings.

There is evidence that he crossed the Bering Bridge and began to spread southwards into the Americas perhaps 30,000 years ago.

And by around 20,000 years ago, it seems that this immensely adventurous and inventive and creative direct ancestor of ours had more or less inherited the entire earth.

This extraordinary idea, strongly supported by many of the world's leading anthropologists including people like Christopher Stringer, of the British Natural History Museum in London, argues that the evidence from the 'bones' is decisive. Namely that this new emigrant, so recent and close to us in our history, simply replaced all previous or existing forms of human being in various parts of the world. He became the single common ancestor of all of today's ethnic groups spread across the continents, however seemingly different they may be, from the Inuit Eskimos in the north to the Patagonian Indians in the south, and from the Polynesian peoples of the Pacific, to the Slavic peoples of eastern Europe. However superficially different the local appearances may be, the fossil evidence indicates that all the varied ethnic groups that we know about share a single common ancestry.

The evidence of a single common ancestry

It is a breath taking idea isn't it, that all the world's peoples are so closely related? Indeed the microbiologists with their study of the DNA and the patterns of gene distribution have been prepared to go further and posit the extraordinary suggestion that we might actually share a common *ancestor*. A female ancestor as it happens. That immediately prompts the question of course of why female? To answer it we need to dip briefly, but interestingly, into the way in which DNA analysis is carried out. Stay with me for just a couple of paragraphs to set it out.

We all carry many metres of DNA material in our bodies. By far the biggest proportion of it, the DNA that dominates the colour of our eyes and the shape of our nose and all the other details of our inheritance from our parents, is tightly coiled inside the *nucleus* of every single cell in the body. Every cell that is, except the sperm and the ova. The DNA in every cell nucleus is a 50/50 blend of the DNA donated by our parents at the moment of conception. So it is *reshuffled* so to speak with every generation. Count back just to your great grandparents say, and you already have your two parents, your four grandparents and your eight great grandparents who have contributed bits to the DNA in the nucleus of each of your cells. Go back even a few generations and the number of contributors rapidly multiplies into the hundreds. So tracing ancestry back over many centuries using this type of DNA is an immensely complex process.

However a relatively small amount of DNA is carried in tiny closed-off capsules inside each cell that are called *mitochondria*. These mitochondria float about in the fluid in each cell. The job of these tiny capsules is to act as fuel converters, converting our food intake into a form of fuel that the body can burn. This little scrap of DNA in the mitochondria, (mtDNA as it is normally abbreviated) has a quite extraordinary and unique quality, in that it is inherited *solely* from the mother. So it isn't constantly reshuffled. It remains the same from generation to generation all the way down the decades, and indeed the centuries. That is to say, the mtDNA in the son's cells, and in the daughter's, is the same as the mtDNA in the mother's cells. It doesn't matter how many generations you go back, ten, twenty, a hundred if you wish, you can still trace your mtDNA directly to your hundred times great great grandmother. That remarkable, unique, *unbroken* thread, passing back in time from generation to generation, has proved to be a huge gift to the scientists trying to track the line that leads back in time, through the passage of the centuries, to our possible distant ancestor, this female ancestor that we've talked about.

Counting the time

There's one other important detail that we need to know to understand the basic outlines of the process. That is that there are tiny, random changes, or mutations as they're called, in this mtDNA that take place over time. Nothing radical, just tiny 'typos' if you like, as it is copied and passed on from generation to generation. These 'typos' or mutations occur at a more or less standard rate, so in a sense they become a sort of ticking clock.

So what does that mean? It is hugely important. It means that by counting up the *differences* between two samples of mtDNA from two different people, it becomes possible to get an accurate fix on how long it has been since these two people shared a *common ancestor.* You can so to speak, measure quite accurately the width of the time gap between them.

Take that idea a step further. Not just two people but many people.

Collect samples of mtDNA from all the main *ethnic groups* around the world; from the North and the South, from the East and the West, from the Americas and Africa, from Europe and Australasia, from the far-flung corners of the world, even from the mountains of Tibet and the deep jungles of New Guinea. That in fact is what has been done, and the cells obtained have been examined under the microscope. By comparing the differences in these far-flung samples of mtDNA it becomes possible to work out two quite extraordinary pieces of information about our distant pre-historic past. The first is how distant is it in *time* since all the different peoples of the earth shared a common ancestor? The second, *where* did that original ancestral group live, from which we are all descended?

Those are two huge questions aren't they? And that is of course a greatly simplified account of the complex process that microbiologists have been going through over the past thirty odd years. Early gene-tracking experiments were first carried out in the late 1970's at Stanford University in California. Increasingly refined techniques have been introduced since, in a whole series of surveys carried out at the Berkeley Campus in California and at Oxford University in England and elsewhere.

We all have African DNA

The weight of the evidence points compellingly towards a conclusion that would have seemed wholly outlandish even a decade or so ago. This extraordinary conclusion is that *everyone* living on earth today, everyone from north to south and east to west, however disparate and different we may seem, is in fact closely related. We all have African DNA in our bodies. We are all descendants from a relatively small group of people, living in East Africa, only this brief while ago in evolutionary terms; the people whose descendants walked out of Africa across the Palestinian Bridge, to appear in Europe around some 40,000 years ago.

Wangari Maathai, the great Kenyan environmentalist and Nobel Peace prize winner has graphically described the implications for how we see ourselves.

'So far all the information we have suggests that we come from somewhere within this part of the World, in East Africa, and that

of course for many people must be surprising because I think we are so used to being divided along ethnic lines or along racial lines, and we look all the time for reasons to be different from each other. So it must be surprising for some of us to realise that what differentiates us is usually very superficial, like the colour of our skins or the colour of our eyes or the texture of our hair. But we are essentially all from the same stem, from the same origin. So I think that as we continue to understand ourselves and appreciate each other, and especially when we get to understand that we all come from the same origin we will shed a lot of the prejudices that we have harboured in the past.'[3]

Isn't that just the most wonderfully positive view of the future?

A new creativity

What is startling is the extent to which these ancestors of ours were so completely different from anything that had come before. So different for example in their sense of individual identity, and in the comparative complexity of the culture they developed. Wherever the archaeologists look they find evidence of a richness and complexity of culture that is breathtaking. This is underlined by the fact that up until that time, just about everything that we know about the nature and the behaviour of primitive human beings has been gleaned from the way that they worked pieces of stone. Suddenly, we have not just totally new stone technologies but art and ornament, and personal jewellery and travel and trade. No wonder it has been described by some archaeologists as a wholly new beginning, a new millennium.

The cave art for example, when it was first discovered, was interpreted simply as a sort of artistic doodling, perhaps the work of bands of hunters, holed up for the long dark winters. Now however, with far more detailed analysis, it is seen to lie at the heart of what must have been carefully planned ritual experiences with powerful social and spiritual implications. Even to reach the site of the paintings would have been a moving experience for most. It would involve summoning up the courage to walk deep into the cold, damp darkness underground, with only the dim light of a flickering oil lamp bouncing off the cave walls, often having to squeeze through narrow passages scarcely wide enough to crawl through, before reaching the cavern or the chamber itself with its brilliantly painted dancing and leaping animal figures. And these painted chambers it has been noted, are often located precisely where ritual chants or shouts would bounce and echo and re-echo off the walls.

The nature and the form of the rituals can only be guessed at; the initiation of the younger members of the tribal family perhaps, or a symbolic re-enactment of the hunt, with the shadows of the hunters looming off the walls. The purpose? Perhaps, to strengthen the spiritual bond that tied all the members of the extended family or tribe who shared in the emotion and the drama of this ritual, deep within the womb of the earth, to enable them to stand more strongly together in the face of the many challenges they undoubtedly had to face beyond the cave.

The emergence of individuality
Moreover apart from the spiritual art, if I may call it that, in the caves, there was a sudden flowering of a wholly new personal art, that clearly played such an important part in the lives of these people. Suddenly there is an exuberance of personal adornment. The fossil graves are rich with items such as necklaces and bracelets and pendants made from

pierced sea shells and carved ivory from the tusks of mammoths. And their significance can be judged from the immense care that has been taken in creating these intensely personal items. Care for example in the selection of only the most exotic sea shells, and care shown in the precision with which the ivory beads of a necklace or a bracelet were painstakingly carved to be exactly the same design on every bead. Each one must have involved literally hours of carving.

As several archaeologists have expressed it, we begin to see in these ancestors of ours something about human nature that hadn't been evident before, and which has continued to become so marked a part of our modern life. Namely the use of objects such as personal ornament, and decoration and even purely utilitarian objects, such as weapons and tools, to convey social messages, to say something clearly to others about the identity and the status and the character of the wearer or the user. The recognition and the demonstration of self has suddenly become an important part of human nature.

The spear thrower is a classic example. It was a short wooden device into which the butt of a dart or a spear could be fitted. By flicking it sharply from over his shoulder it worked rather like a sling shot; the hunter could give much greater acceleration to his dart as it speeds towards the bison or the ibex he has been tracking. It works no more nor no less efficiently of course, whether it is carved and decorated, or just a plain piece of wood. The decoration only matters if the sense of *personal identity* has become a central fact in the owner's life. And it seems that it had. That profound change is evidenced for the first time amongst these people. What had once been purely utilitarian, simply tools or weapons, become carriers of social messages. The beautifully carved and shaped spear thrower with elaborate markings along its sides, or perhaps with a miniature ibex carved delicately out of one end, tells us as much about the personality of the hunter at whose side it hung, as it does about the technique of hunting.

The desire for connection

When archaeologists scratch their heads and ponder the reason for this remarkable, revolutionary change in the style and way of life of these people who, in a few short centuries became us, one of the dominant reasons they point to, is their extraordinary ability to make connections, right across the face of Europe. Where once there had been stasis and isolation, small family groups hunkered down in relatively small areas of territory, somewhere by a river or in a deep valley, now there is movement and travel and trade and communication, and no doubt alliance and intermarriage.

The evidence for the emergence and flowering of movement and trade is everywhere. Stone for example begins to travel. Whereas immediately prior to the arrival of our ancestors into Europe tools were made almost entirely from types of stone found in the immediate vicinity. Suddenly, cutting tools and spear points are made from the best stone available, even when it has to be carried from a hundred or more miles away. Sea shells that existed only on the Mediterranean shore, are found in necklaces and bracelets at sites in the distant north. Ivory from the north is found as carved beads at sites in the Dordogne in the south. And it seems clear that people sought out whatever was most foreign and most exotic. People who lived where shells were abundant didn't want shells, they traded them for the ivory that came from afar. And vice versa. There are even examples that have been found of ivory carved to *look like* pierced sea shells. Why would that be, except to give it this extra dimension of the rare and the exotic?

If that is the case it does have a resoundingly modern ring to it, and the implications of these kinds of discoveries would seem to demand a radical re-thinking of the kinds of lives these people lived, and the kinds of concerns and motivations that drove their lives. Their lives must have been in all too many ways nasty, brutish and short. But it seems clear that they had concerns that went well beyond just eking out a hard-won and primitive existence.

If we turn to the archaeologists, they tell us that this willingness to adventure on the part of our immediate forebears, this desire to reach out and connect with far flung tribes and families had a profound effect upon their entire way of life, and the sheer speed with which their ideas and their technologies evolved and travelled.

If we turn to the psychologists, they tell us that it goes rather further than that. It also tells us, they say, much about the *inner life* of these people. That what we are witnessing is in effect the rapid growth and development of the human mind, of human consciousness. You would scarcely expect something as fundamentally elusive as consciousness to show up in the fossil record, and of course it doesn't. What does show up however, as we have seen, is its manifestation in action, the sheer scale of the movement and inter-connection that took place across territories and across continents. Movement and trade inevitably mean encounters with strangers, and, the psychologists argue, those encounters must have presented perhaps the greatest challenges these people were likely to face. Why? Because it was a new type of challenge, never before encountered on such a large scale. To be successful the traveller had to become in effect, a mind reader.

The physical dangers presented by forests and cliffs, by gorges and icy mountain torrents may have presented many challenges, and indeed taken many lives, but the nature of the challenges were well known. As indeed were the likely threats from wild animals, since they were a part of every hunter-gatherer's life. But every stranger presented a quite different challenge, a wholly unknown quantity. The successful traveller-trader had to learn how to read a stranger's mind, with its immense capacity for cunning and deceit as well as for friendship and alliance. Friend or foe, welcoming or threatening, trustworthy or deceiving. His life might well depend upon getting that reading right. This time. And next time. And the time after.

The psychologist Nicholas Humphrey, in his book *The Inner Eye*,[4] suggests that the response that our ancestors came up with was the growth in the power of 'introspection.' By learning to look within our *own* minds he suggests, we developed the ability to read something of what is going on within the minds of others, from the tiniest physical signals transmitted without; through the flickering of the eyes for example, or the slightest movement of the muscles around the mouth, or the tightening of the muscles in the neck, and so on. By developing our ability to peer within our own minds, to see more of our own consciousness, to read our own impulses and motivations and reactions, so we gain a greater insight into the minds, and therefore into the actions of others.

All that having been said, the evolution of consciousness remains a deep mystery. There is no doubt that *it is* a product of evolution, although no one is in a position to say when or indeed how consciousness evolved. The field is wide open. Some evolutionary biologists are prepared to argue that it existed in some form among gorillas and chimpanzees and other primates and indeed other species, wolves and hunting dogs and big cats, long before man appeared on the evolutionary tree. Many of us are aware that we can be pretty easily manipulated by the responses of our dog or our cat. I know one man who declares that he is frequently manipulated by his parrot! So it is difficult indeed to imagine that they don't have a pretty well developed sense of self. Others scientists however, continue to maintain that the appearance of consciousness in a form that we would recognise as *modern*, is a far more recent event, appearing perhaps only shortly before the dawn of agricultural communities.

A time line from then to today

But in the midst of this mystery, what seems clear is that the moment when our ancestors chose to walk out of Africa must have been a major horizon in the development of the consciousness that we recognise and seek to understand today. It was only after that event that we begin to see the emergence, and the acceleration, in the development of so much that we regard as essential to the nature of our modern human-ness. We may see it only in *objects,* since only objects survive the passing of the centuries. The images of the horses galloping wildly across the cave walls at Lascaux. The care that has gone into the making of the ivory necklace. The intricate carving of the ibex on the handle of the personalised spear thrower. But the objects speak clearly to us of the emergence and development of subtle relationships between human beings, and of a complexity of consciousness that we had not witnessed before.

And quite remarkably, it is possible I think, to carve a time line that bridges directly from that day to this. From the wild paintings on the wall at Lascaux for example to the top of Headington Hill in Oxford. We could bridge to several other places in the world, but Headington Hill will do, because there sits the home of Oxford University Neuroscience, a world-leading centre of research into who we are and how our minds and brains work. Their web site tells us simply, that

'... it is at the forefront of one of the greatest challenges of the 21st century; deciphering how the brain works.' And...it goes on...hoping to understand one day, 'perhaps even how brains generate consciousness.'[5]

That word 'even' is a crucial giveaway isn't it? In that it immediately gives us a measure of the huge achievement that would represent, understanding the *nature* of consciousness, even today. We have no idea how it is that the movement of measurable and *material* things, things like electrical signals along the neurons in the brain and the movement of chemical messengers across the synapses, becomes translated into the immeasurable and the immaterial and emotional, the deeply intimate sense of a self, living at the centre of an extraordinary world. But we do know of course that consciousness is deeply involved in our sense of happiness and suffering. Buddhism for example, has always taught the immensely hope-filled principle that both suffering and happiness come not, as we so commonly believe, from the external factors in our lives, but from deep within. And that's where we go next, to look at what religion is all about

—∙∙∙∙—

CHAPTER THREE

So What's Religion all About?

It is quite a substantial leap from human evolution to religion, but it is the leap we make now because it plays such a key role, and occupies so many dimensions on the journey we are making. The extraordinary nature of religion is that it is everywhere. Even if personally we choose to make little or no space for religion in our lives, we encounter it wherever we look in human civilisation, and however far back we look. There is no period that we can point to when it wasn't present. Whenever we use the word, for the vast mass of the world's population it will conjure up some potent image or memory, because it is almost impossible for us not to have encountered a religion of sorts in our upbringing, from the simplicity of a school assembly perhaps, to the experience of a funeral or a church wedding, and on to the soaring magnificence of the dome of St. Peter's Basilica in Rome, or the evening cry of the muezzin from his minaret in dusty down town Jeddah. And it has a powerful role to play in even the remotest corners that we can imagine.

When I travelled all those years ago deep into the highlands of Borneo, spending the nights swapping life stories with families of Dayaks in the dim light of their longhouses, they took great care always to place gifts of rice and other food on little platforms alongside the narrow pathways that led into the dense and trackless jungle, and at the boundaries of their small and scattered fields. It was one way among several to express their constant awareness of the many forces around them which, they believed, had such a powerful influence on their lives. On the growth of their crops for example, or the fertility of their pigs scrabbling in the dirt under the longhouse. So this awareness was an important part of the structure within which they lived their lives, and hence an important part of their sense of the order of things and of their well being. And of course we should remember that no one had created this sense for them, or imposed it upon them.

In his wonderful book, *Don't Sleep there are Snakes*, Daniel Everett, missionary and linguist, tells us that when he lived for a while as a missionary among the Piraha Indians in the central Amazon jungle, the Indians constantly claimed to *see* their gods in person, and as a regular occurrence, flitting swiftly among the trees, or standing across from them on some sandy river shore. And they weren't just there, just *being,* so to speak. The Indians would recount in graphic detail how these gods would be shouting important information or advice or warnings to them. And the tribesmen simply couldn't understand how this clever American stranger in their midst was so blind, so insensitive, so disconnected from their reality, that he could see nothing, when they could see the friendly and familiar figure of the gods so clearly. It was, as Daniel expresses it, a startling revelation of two widely different views of what constitutes reality, arising directly from two quite different sets of belief. With his solid, deep-seated Christian vision he simply didn't have the eyes to *see* the important and familiar gods of these Amazonian Indians.[1]

Incidentally Daniel goes on to tell us that as he became more aware of the fullness of these people's lives, and their complete sense of oneness and communion with their environment, the *seeing* of the gods was simply a practical manifestation of that, his personal sense of mission gradually faded away. It became somehow irrelevant. He no longer had any desire to move these people into any other area of belief.

A deeply rooted aspect of human nature

These examples also make a crucially important point that we ought not to pass by. It is noteworthy that these tribes, although they live out their lives so remotely, without contact with any other civilisation, they still come up with as powerful an expression of religion in their daily lives, as for example, societies from more crowded areas of the globe that live shoulder to shoulder with other cultures, and so have a profound effect upon one another. That is, I would suggest, at the very least an indication that the religious inclination is a deeply rooted aspect of all human nature. It seems indeed that there might even be an *instinct* for religion, if I may express it that way. Certainly the religious dimension has been described by some historians as one of the primary axes upon which the evolution of human culture has turned.

That idea in turn clearly raises some important questions for us doesn't it? Why, we have to ask, is religion found at the heart of almost every human culture? Where does it come from? What role does it play? The questions have been around for a long time of course, but the extraordinary fact is that the interest in them seems to be growing rather than diminishing. In fact it has led to an increasing flurry of research and debate over the past ten years or so, not simply among theologians, but among a widening group of scientists, from evolutionary biologists to sociologists and psychologists.

So far from fading away, as the modern stereotype would suggest, it is clear that for around two thirds of the world's population, their religious convictions and the values they embody have a central role to play in their daily lives, and therefore in their sense of completeness and well being.

The benefits

In fact, even if we leave aside from this discussion anything to do with belief, if I may call it that, there is very considerable research evidence to suggest that on a purely personal basis, a religious dimension in our lives does bring with it considerable benefits. It would seem to be a definite plus rather than a minus. Psychologist Professor Martin Seligman for example, from the University of Pennsylvania, places a religious belief among the most important factors in enabling us to establish a strong and resilient sense of stability and well being in our lives.[2] Dr. Andrew Newberg, who is a psychiatrist and a research director at the Thomas Jefferson Hospital and Medical School, argues that, *'A large body of science shows a positive impact of religion on health.'*[3]

Similarly, Dr. Herbert Benson, Professor of Medicine at Harvard Medical School, conducted a long series of clinical studies in the 1990's into the relationship between various forms of prayer and religious practice, and our ability to overcome various forms of stress and anxiety and illness. The results of those studies are set out in detail in his account, *Timeless Healing, the Power and Biology of Belief.* His conclusion, essentially, is that many forms of prayer, provided they arise from a well-founded religious belief, have powerful and immensely beneficial effects on critical physiological factors such as blood pressure and stable heart rates and heightened immune systems. He argues that this kind of prayer, used on a regular basis, and hinged to fundamental belief systems, has been shown conclusively to help people recover from their illness or their operation or their unhappiness, more rapidly and more completely, and often against the most difficult odds. Dr. Benson coined a memorable phrase to define this belief-based healing process. He described it as returning to *'remembered wellness.'* And clearly, wellness, in all its dimensions, plays a crucially important role in happiness.[4]

Where civilisation begins

Those kinds of conclusions, backed by the results of properly conducted scientific surveys and analyses, are of course a wholly modern phenomenon. But one might argue perhaps that there has been at least some understanding at a far deeper subconscious level, of the benefits that have come from religious belief for well...for millennia. How else explain the universality of religion as a powerful and dynamic factor, shaping every human culture that we have knowledge of, and as far back as we can see. Social historians such as the late Arnold Toynbee for example talk of religion as being at the very heart of civilisation, providing the fundamental *spiritual* energy if you like, that brought successive civilisations into being and then sustained them, often for thousands of years.[5]

The cycle involved has many familiar elements. Leaving aside the sort of rituals that took place deep in the caves of Southern France, as far as we can tell the religious experience begins, essentially where civilisation begins, in the green and fertile crescent between the Tigris and the Euphrates, around some 10,000 years ago. Peoples who had once been nomads began to settle into stable farming communities, and we see the growth of the world's first villages and then towns and then the cities, whose names occur in the early chapters of the Old Testament, names such as Babylon and Uruk and Ur.

What seems to have happened was that as soon as a community was able to create a surplus of food and of other resources beyond the basic survival level, then part of that surplus was dedicated to the establishment of a religious dimension in their lives. The little gifts of offerings and food that we saw on the tracks outside the Dayak longhouse grow in scale, to become the creation of an active priesthood, and the construction of religious buildings that had no other practical use. So they represented a substantial allocation or investment, of the whole community's wealth and resources. An investment that could only have been achieved, the historians argue, with the willingness, and the social harmony and the energy that came from a commonly held religious belief that was shared throughout all levels in a society.

In all the succession of civilisations that sprang up over the succeeding millennia, in all the great river systems of the world, such as the Euphrates and the Nile, the Danube and the Indus, the Ganges and the Yangtze, they all had powerful religious systems embedded in their culture. And the key point surely, is that this is true not for *some* of these civilisations, but for all of them. Indeed when today we search through the scattered fragmentary remains of these past civilisations, it is striking that it is this religious dimension that has often left the most abundant relics, and so often those that are the most revealing of the way of life. Moreover we can't ignore the dominant fact that religions didn't come cheaply. At every turn they devoured huge amounts of time and labour and energy and wealth to establish and to maintain.

So what fundamentally is religion about?

To the religious believer, that question might seem to be pretty much an irrelevance. Since the religion was seen to sit at the very centre of the way society worked, it wasn't so much a question of choice, as of *acceptance* by the body of believers.

If we turn to the historians and the evolutionary scientists for guidance, they view that religious heritage through a very specialised lens of course, a social and evolutionary lens, rather than a spiritual one. Rather like anthropologist Daniel Everett, rendered sightless among the Indians in the Amazon jungle, they can't actually *see* the gods. What they do see is religion as very much an *evolutionary adaptation* to the wholly new environment of the agricultural civilisations as they emerged. It was they argue, a crucially important part of the way in which people and societies learned how to *live together*, as they settled down to live more settled, communal lives in these great fertile valleys. An evolutionary adaptation they argue, not immensely different from that of learning how to sow and reap crops, and develop trade; a way of enabling an increasingly complex and settled society to work harmoniously.

David Sloan Wilson for example, a prominent evolutionary biologist, argues that the main evolutionary benefit of religion was that it provided the most powerful *bonding mechanism* at the centre of society. It underpinned and sustained the sense of belonging to the same society and sharing in the social cohesion that resulted. This was crucially important, he argues, at a time of rapid transition to a settled urban and agricultural way of life that brought all kinds of new social challenges.[6]

But what about the spiritual experience?

That kind of analysis may well be wholly accurate, but I have to say that I find it rather less than satisfying as a meaningful way of looking at people living their daily lives, not least because it seems to take little account of the actual *spiritual* experience of the individual.

One might argue therefore that, whatever the well-spring of the religion, what it provided above all else, was a sense of a deeper meaning and purpose to people's lives. A sense of structure and stability. A vision of a higher reality that lay above and beyond the dirt and the squalor and the toil and the pain of ordinary daily life. Whatever your view might be of the rightness or otherwise of the religious belief itself, those purposes are clearly immensely important ones, central to the well-being of the individual, and crucial to the harmony of the society of which they were a member. Evolutionary psychologists do indeed talk of a sense of 'elevation,' lifting people beyond their own immediate personal interests on to a wider, more communal, more co-operative, more selfless plane.

Where are we heading?

Fast forward a few thousand years, and it has left us of course, that immense religious heritage, with the immense richness of the religions we have amongst us today, Hinduism and Buddhism and Sikhism and Judaism and Christianity and Islam, and many more, all of which have their deepest roots in these ancient civilisations.

Arnold Toynbee, gives us an interesting glimpse of the direction in which, he believes, that rich religious tradition is moving.

'It looks to me as if a union of the higher religions is already beginning to take place. As I see it this union is taking the form not of unification, but of a mutual recognition that each of these religions has a distinctive and unique, though only partial vision

of ultimate reality and that all of them are valuable for mankind. Different human beings have different temperaments besides having different experiences. Since there are different variations on our common human nature, it is fortunate that there should be more than one vision of ultimate reality to help us catch a glimmer of understanding'[7]

' *…to help us catch a glimmer of understanding.'* Such a brilliant phrase. It underlines so powerfully the immense difficulty we all have in grasping the true nature of the human condition that lies behind the mundane muddle of our daily lives, and religion he argues, plays a central role in helping us towards such an understanding.

That is undoubtedly a strong and positive view of the role that religion continues to play in our lives. But there are also powerful contrary views that we ought to look at albeit briefly.

Arguments for and against

So let's tackle the very toughest challenges that are commonly marshalled against religion, and two it seems to me stand out above the rest. One is that religion has led over the centuries to as much harm as it has good, in the sense that it has been the cause of countless atrocities throughout history. The second is that the claims that religion makes are not verifiable or measurable and therefore out of place in a rational and scientific age.

Let's consider both of those issues as briefly as I dare, and still make sense of the arguments.

Religion is inhuman?

It is of course undeniable that religion in its various modes, has been the professed inspiration of very considerable atrocities down the centuries. The list is a long one. From the ritual slaughters carried out by the knights of the Crusades and the many executions carried out by the Inquisition in the name of the Christian God, to today's long campaign of suicide bombers against thousands of wholly innocent people, committed in the name of the Islamic Jihad. There can be no rationale to excuse these excesses, carried out in the name of religion, or under the banner of the pursuit of religious freedom.

The most powerful argument that historians introduce to redress the balance so to speak, is that if you look at human history it is filled to overflowing with examples of man's gross inhumanity to man, committed in the name of many causes? And it is undeniably part of our modern tragedy, part of our modern failing, that there seems to be no let up in their occurrence. The professed causes are many. Religion is among them of course, but so too are Fascism and Marxism, Racism, Science even, since that lay at the root of much that was committed both by the Nazi regime and by the white supremacists in South Africa, and elsewhere. Auschwitz they argue, was not primarily a religious event, nor was Apartheid. They were both driven by wholly misguided and extreme views of racial superiority. While today, as has been said on many occasions by many Islamic scholars, Jihadists would seem to be driven by political rather than religious motives, whatever they may profess.

So take away religion. Remove it from the scene. Ban it by government edict. What do we end up with? We are still left with The Final Solution. The Soviet Massacres. The Killing Fields of Cambodia. And Apartheid. And Rwanda. And Darfur, and many other unspeakable events. In his recent book *Falling off the Edge* for example, Alex Perry makes the powerful case that Darfur and Rwanda are clear examples of resource wars. At their heart he argues, they are about water and about grass, more than they are about racial tension.[8]

But the key point I wish to make is clear, namely that eradicating religion, would not, as has been claimed so frequently, provide a *solution* to these acts of brutality between men. It is going too far perhaps to suggest that religion is almost irrelevant in this context, but the root cause is clearly much more to do with a profound fear of the other. Ignorance, distrust, fear, loathing, hatred, of that which is different from oneself or one's tribal or ethnic grouping. The ignorance and the distrust and the fear show themselves in many forms, from simply not wishing to associate with these other people, through to rejection of their culture, and on to its most extreme manifestation, the desire to destroy them.

Is there a solution?

Sadly there is nothing yet in this situation resembling a solution, but there is what one might call a clear direction, most powerfully set out perhaps in Buddhist teachings, with their clearly professed aim of achieving global peace, by working continuously and patiently towards reducing and then eliminating, the ignorance and the distrust and the fear and loathing and hatred of the other.

Indeed, if we look at the huge challenges confronting us today, such as global warming and climate change and population growth and acute shortages of food and fresh water and so on, they have led some social commentators to observe that Buddhism could be said to offer a kind of *universal promise* in this 21st Century, in the sense that since it is not attached to any definition if divinity, it doesn't create or recognise any *boundaries.* It is wholly inclusive. Nothing and no one is excluded. The only qualification if you like is to be a member of the human race. And what undoubtedly distinguishes these modern problems from so many challenges in the past is that they are truly global, they embrace all of us, the entire human race. They pay no heed to ethnic or racial or religious or national boundaries, or indeed partial distinctions of any kind.

It is in that sense then, that it has been argued that since Buddhism is alone in offering a religious model that *transcends* all the existing boundaries that stand between national and racial and religious groupings, it could well deliver the religious model the world needs, as it faces these huge challenges in the next hundred years.

You can't prove religion

That really brings us to the second major charge levelled against religion, namely that it is not in large measure verifiable. That is of course true. Absolutely. You can't measure religious or spiritual belief, any more than you can measure the things that religion is interested in, such as love and hate, or courage and compassion. Religions are based essentially upon the profound insights and reflections of religious thinkers and philosophers about the nature of ultimate reality, and the significance of human life. Why are we here? Is there a purpose and a meaning to our life? What is the significance of our spiritual awareness? What happens to us after death?

As we have seen, we don't aim those questions at science, for the obvious reason that such answers as we can arrive at, are not verifiable in a strictly scientific sense. But that does not mean of course that the questions themselves are not *real or meaningful to us.* Indeed they can be among the most important questions we will ever ask in our lives. Just as the answers we receive, can have the most valuable and creative impact on the way we approach our daily lives.

I am reminded of a powerful argument on this very issue put forward by Arnold Toynbee in the book I quoted from a little earlier, entitled *Choose Life.* Professor Toynbee argues,

'Scientists limit their objectives to observing phenomena, seeking to explain them rationally and trying to test their conclusions. In contrast to science religion offers human beings a chart of the mysterious world in which we awoke to consciousness and in which we have to pass our lives. Although this chart is conjectural, we cannot do without it. It is the necessity of life. It is of far greater importance for us than most of science's tested and certified surveys of the tiny fraction of the universe that is accessible to us for scientific exploration.'[9]

The line at the heart of that passage, *'Although this chart is conjectural, we cannot do without it. It is the necessity of life.'* clearly expresses the very essence of the argument of this Chapter. It takes us back to that key difference we touched upon earlier; we ask of science the question, is it right, since that is the nature of the claim that scientists make for their findings, an addition to our precise knowledge of the universe we inhabit. But by the same token, we are perfectly entitled to ask of religion a quite different question, namely does it help us to live a richer life? Does it enable us to chart our way through the complexities of life more effectively, and with a greater sense of fulfilment and wholeness?

At that basic, daily, human level it is difficult indeed to understand why this old argument that we loosely call science versus religion hasn't been put to bed years ago. We so clearly need both sources of inspiration. Arnold Toynbee once again, points us towards the essential truth,,

'Science and religion need not and ought not to be in conflict. They are two complementary ways of approaching the universe mentally in order to cope with it'[10]

And Einstein I would argue, in his famous dictum, got it just about spot on. Science without religion *is lame*, it positively limps along if it seeks to present itself as a complete explanation and description of our full humanity. Religion similarly *is blind*, if it believes it can ignore the rich and extraordinary insights into the nature of human motivation and behaviour provided by the sciences.

So if we are to establish a solid basis for making the very most of our lives in this remarkable universe that we inhabit, I would suggest the case is clear, we have an *absolute need* for the very different kinds of illumination and understanding that come from both science and religion. Both are crucial. We should therefore stand up and take serious issue with the scientists whenever they choose to argue that our lives would be richer without the religious bit. In doing so we can enlist the support of some powerful allies down the centuries, writers and scientists and poets and philosophers, and not least among them the creator of Buddhism, Shakyamuni Buddha himself,

—ɯ—

CHAPTER FOUR

What's so Special about Buddhism?

What is so special about Buddhism is that it is a man made religion. It is a profound vision of the nature and purpose of human life from one ordinary human being, albeit a man with immense wisdom and perception, as well of course as an extraordinary ability to communicate his profound ideas, passed on to all other ordinary human beings, *on the basis of equality.*

Thus there is no divine hierarchy in Buddhism. It is this characteristic above all that gives Buddhism its wholly distinctive character. Rather than being a set of dogma and beliefs, handed down to mankind in various ways by a divine presence or being, Buddhism is firmly rooted from first to last, in ordinary humanity. It is about every man's relationship with himself, and with his fellow human beings. The commandments of a divine being brook no debate you might say, whereas the vision of life presented by another human being demands it. As Edward Conze, from Cambridge, one of the most distinguished scholars of Buddhism has written in his history of the religion,

'The Buddha always stressed that he was a guide, not an authority, and that all religious propositions must be tested, including his own.'[1]

And since the most basic of human desires has to do with happiness in this life, so Buddhism is essentially about the transformation of those things that cause us so much pain and anguish in life, such as self doubt and anxiety and fear, fear of so many things, fear of failure, fear of loss, fear of rejection, fear of inadequacy.

Transformation into what you might ask? And the somewhat surprising answer is, into the very stuff of happiness itself, into the achievement of a deep-rooted, strongly-based, stable sense of well being at the heart of one's life. Moreover Buddhism goes further, it encourages us constantly with the life-transforming idea that the achievement of that goal is a matter of choice rather than a matter of chance or accident, as we commonly tend to believe or assume. Hope if you like becomes a *determination* rather than just a wish. That is to say, we have the ability to determine that we want to live in this way, and that we can learn how to set about achieving it. In that sense Buddhism might be described, without in any way diminishing it, as the ultimate self help process.

There is another distinctive quality that we touched upon briefly earlier, but it is so important it bears repetition, namely that since Buddhism is not attached to any definition of divinity, and doesn't have any boundaries, it is wholly inclusive. And in this sense it is a colossal vision. It reaches out in ever widening circles to embrace and to illuminate every man's relationship with himself, man and his relationship with society, society and the environment, the environment and the Universe.

These key elements of personal choice and of unbounded inclusiveness are perhaps the key qualities that give Buddhism its universal appeal and its astounding, everlasting modernity. It may have begun in the Deer Park in the little town of Sarnath in Northern India, when Shakyamuni first sat down to talk to a small group of people about his newly-won ideas all those years ago, but in no sense is it ancient, in no sense is it stuck in time. In no way is it about the past. For each generation it continues to prove itself to be always about the here and the now of life.

The life of Shakyamuni Buddha

All Buddhist teachings stem essentially from the life experience of Shakyamuni Buddha. He is the seed from which this great tree has grown. His teachings have changed the course of world history in so many ways, but he lived at a time when nothing was written down, so relatively little is known about his long life story. And as you might expect, it's often difficult to distinguish between historical fact and the many myths and legends that have grown up around so large a life.

The distinctive fact at the centre of his life is however completely clear; he was throughout his life rooted firmly in this world. Unlike Jesus and Mohammed, he didn't claim any kind of divine connection, or that his teachings had a divine inspiration. He was born the son of the ruling family of the Shakya tribe or clan, hence the name Shakya-muni, or 'Sage of the Shakyas'. This small kingdom lay on the borders of modern-day Nepal. His birth is normally placed at around 500BCE. The precise date is not vitally important, but the period is, because within the space of little more than 100 years a number of great radical thinkers were creating an extraordinary tide of revolutionary ideas about the nature of human life, right across the known world, from Socrates in Greece, and Isaiah in Israel to Shakyamuni in India and Confucius in China. As a result this period of immense intellectual ferment has been described as the dawn of our spiritual civilisation; a brief period that produced many of the spiritual ideas that have played so big a role in human motivation and behaviour ever since.

Shakyamuni as the eldest son would have been groomed to take over the kingdom from his father at some stage, and he seems to have lived a life of some seclusion in the palace, having little contact with the world of poverty and hardship beyond the walls. Apart from that he seems to have lived an ordinary if somewhat affluent life. He married around the age of 16 and had a son, who later became one of his leading disciples. But Shakyamuni was clearly no ordinary man. Quite suddenly, when he was in his late 20's according to the most widely accepted tradition, he decided to break away from the life path that had been established for him and leave his father's house, and his young family. He committed himself from that moment to what he saw as a search for the truth, for answers to the fundamental questions about the nature and the significance and the ultimate reality of human life. And indeed death. A decision made by one man, living in obscurity in a small town in Northern India, that has since changed the lives of many millions of people down the ages.

What was it that drove him to make such a radical departure? We don't really know. We do know that though unusual, it wasn't wholly unprecedented. It seems that in some cases the eldest sons in privileged households in India at this time might well go into the wilderness so to speak, to pursue the path of enlightenment, at least for a period of time, rather than immediately follow in their father's footsteps into a political or commercial career. Although few can have followed this path with the passion and the commitment that Shakyamuni displayed. And in his case tradition provides us with a very clear motivation. It seems that when he became aware of the sheer scale of the suffering and the hardship of ordinary men and women in the real world outside the palace walls, he simply could not ignore it. He was driven to take some action, to seek to save mankind if you will. He gave up everything he had, and set of, essentially to find some way of transcending or dealing with, the sufferings that are so clearly inherent in human life.

It's important to hang on to the fact that this is the essential starting point of the Buddhist religion, the mystery, or the *dilemma of human suffering.* The mystery locked up in the questions, what is human life about? What gives rise to human suffering? How can we best deal with it? How can we find a pathway to greater happiness in the midst of life's difficulties? They are questions that challenge us just as powerfully today of course, despite our vastly greater affluence and insulation against life's troubles. We may choose not to look at them, or not to recognise them, particularly if we happen to be in the midst of our youthful life, but as Job reminds us from another religious tradition, at whatever stage we are in the journey, troubles do lie thick and fast around us; 'Man is born to troubles as the sparks fly upwards,' he tells us. And the reality of his message is born out a hundredfold in every day's newspaper headlines, every single day. Indeed it might well be argued that man invented religion, in his own image so to speak, as one way of coping with the teeming troubles of daily life.

A time of great change

It helps as well I think, to know something about the environment into which Shakyamuni went, to pursue his search for greater understanding of the human condition, because it was a time of transition and change. He grew up in a society that was utterly dominated by a Brahman priestly class, which wielded an almost divine authority. They did so as the representatives on earth of a powerful pantheon of gods who ruled over the affairs of men. To avoid the wrath of the gods was a daily concern for everyone at every level.

But there were new and powerful forces that were beginning to break the patterns of the older tribal society, built around centuries of this Brahman religious authority. There was a huge increase in commerce and trade for example in Northern India, leading to the rise of a new, rich and influential merchant class, and the growth of larger towns and cities. People began to move in considerable numbers from the close- knit rural communities, where they were bound together by the ancient traditions, into the richer towns and cities, where family and tribal ties were looser. So there were the beginnings of a rootless, disconnected urban society. Above all perhaps the authority of the Brahman priestly class, which had underpinned the social structure for centuries, was being openly challenged. Ordinary people were seeking greater religious and intellectual freedoms.

His time in the wilderness

It must have been with an awareness of the growing challenge to long-established social and religious structures that Shakyamuni spent several years in what might be called his own personal wilderness, travelling his own inner journey. He was still a young man and he went through an intense period of spiritual evolution, as he explored what were held then to be the most likely routes towards personal enlightenment, or the deepest understanding of life.

Even the greatest revolutionaries are to some extent prisoners of their time, and the conventional routes to self-knowledge were held to be profound meditation and extreme asceticism. These were the routes that Shakyamuni initially explored. We are told that he attached himself to two of the most advanced teachers in yogic meditation until he himself had attained their level of awakening or concentration; 'the place where nothing exists,' as it has been described. Then he departed, realising, according to the texts that describe this period of his life, that these kinds of practices, did indeed lead to reduction in earthly desires, but the result was a kind of emptiness. They had little to offer therefore, for an ordinary person trying to eke out an existence in a tough and challenging world. They became in a sense, a sort of cul de sac, an end in themselves. They led not so much to a richer life as to a reduction of life, to 'the place where nothing exists.'

Shakyamuni moved on to a period where he is described as putting himself through the most severe ascetic practices or austerities, as they were called, involving acts like suspension of breathing almost to the point of unconsciousness, and prolonged fasting. In a sense the underlying motivation is very close to that of extreme meditation, the denial of the body in order to free the mind. If the body weighs down the spirit, and blocks the upward progress of the mind towards spiritual enlightenment, then in some way that bond must be broken. The body must be denied and the spirit left free to fly. That profound dualism is not of course restricted to ancient Brahmanism. It is with us today in several forms. Indeed many people will recognise some element of this mind-body dualism, or conflict even, in modern Christianity. Giving up something you particularly like for Lent for example is a somewhat oblique relic of the same idea. My own name bears witness to its prevalence in Medieval Christianity; 'going woolward' described the common practice of wearing a rough and intensely irritating hair shirt next to the skin, for monks or friars who had broken the rules of their order, and therefore were punishing themselves.

But for Shakyamuni, he was clearly prepared to push himself to the very limit, to taste the pain and anguish of deep bodily suffering in order to grasp the meaning of spiritual freedom. So he tested these forms of extreme bodily denial to the ultimate before he was able to accept that this could not be the path to the liberation of the spirit that he was seeking. Essentially we're told that he came to realise that these punishing practices were simply wrecking his body, and limiting, rather than heightening his ability to think clearly and take positive action. He moved on. He began to build up his body again, and he began to meditate anew.

Shakyamuni's enlightenment

What exactly happened to Shakyamuni during his long period of meditation as tradition has it, under the Bodhi tree near the village of Buddhagaya, is hard to understand, and even harder to describe, in a way that makes it wholly accessible to the modern inquirer. If you go to Buddhagaya today it is strangely reminiscent of going to say Bethlehem in Palestine. It is still a simple village in all its elements. Ordinary mundane life goes on there in all the dust and disarray. But there is also a sense of being at a place where history has changed direction, even though we can't understand quite why.

It goes without saying that we do find it difficult to understand precisely what happened to Shakyamuni, in very much the same way that we find it difficult to understand what happened to the Christian persecutor Saul, on the road to Damascus, that turned him into St. Paul, the greatest missionary and the primary architect of the Christian Church. These moments of extreme revelation or enlightenment in *individual* lives, that go on to change the whole direction of human history, are, by definition, rare and deeply mystical in the truest sense of that word. They are genuinely beyond the reach of the intellect.

However, I don't think that should surprise us, or frustrate us in any way, since almost by definition, a state of being or a state of mind labelled 'enlightenment' is bound to be strange, not to say alien to us. It's a word that we are not likely to use very often, if at all. In an essentially intellectual and materialist age we are much more comfortable with matter-of-fact explanations, and scientific patterns of proof, than we are with mystical experiences. We have to accept I think that we can only go so far; that in using an unusual word like 'enlightenment,' we are reaching out in an attempt to describe something that may be very difficult to pin down, but which remains nonetheless, a wholly valid part of human experience.

Whatever the precise nature of the truths about human existence that Shakyamuni perceived, whatever the elements of the story that we find difficult to believe, or to understand, because of the limitations of our own experience or imagination, such historical facts as there are seem clear enough. The essential point to hang onto is that the immense, moving power of the experience lit a fire in Shakyamuni's heart that was never extinguished. It launched him into a lifetime of endeavour from which he was never able to pull back. Like St. Paul after his experience on the road to Damascus, Shakyamuni was never again able to separate his daily existence as a human being, from his teaching of the truths that he had experienced, even to the very moment of his death.

The great dilemma

The great dilemma facing Shakyamuni, was the dilemma that faces all great visionaries throughout history, namely how to move on after his transcendent experience? How to convey the essence of what he had learned, in ways that could be readily grasped and understood by ordinary people, so as to make a practical difference to their lives? And right at the heart of his teaching was the clear message that the new understanding that he had gained of human life and motivation, although radical and unusual in its direction and its implications, it was not in any sense *divine,* or in any way *separate from* the patterns of ordinary human existence. How could it be since *he* was no more, nor no less than that, an ordinary human being? What he had experienced was simply the highest reach of an ordinary human mind.

He was a clearly a man of great charisma and an inspirational teacher, and whatever he had to say undoubtedly touched people's lives closely. It wasn't in that sense remote and academic. Basically his teaching eliminated any idea of a pantheon of gods who controlled human destiny. It was concerned solely with the growth and liberation of the individual human spirit. So it was about each man's relationship to himself and his own life, and how he related to those whom his life touched. Over the long period of his teaching, he steadily evolved and deepened this powerful human-centred philosophy, and it was this profound humanism that touched and drew in people from all backgrounds and all walks of life, from beggars to merchants, from craftsmen to kings, from farmers to philosophers.

They all wanted to see him, and hear him speak in person. So wherever he went people flocked to listen. He didn't teach enlightenment so much as he taught healing and hope, and above all perhaps how to see life differently in coping with day-to-day difficulties, how to handle sickness and despair, how to overcome the destructive passions of fear and anger and hatred. Over the long lifetime of his mission, he taught always at a level that could be received and understood by his audience. His concern was to take his audience with him up what might be called a staircase of understanding, since his teaching was radical in the extreme, particularly when seen against the centuries-long background of Brahmanism.

The gift of choice

It is difficult to write a simple coda on so big a life, but it has been argued by religious historians that perhaps Buddhism's greatest gift to mankind's religious or spiritual history, is that it introduced the concept of *choice.* At a time when people saw themselves as being hemmed in by powerful, controlling and limiting concepts such as destiny and the will of the gods, Shakyamuni introduced this extraordinary idea that we are truly answerable only to ourselves. We have the freedom, and the resource, to make our own choices, to take control over our lives, provided only that we accept full responsibility for the choices that we personally make, and their implications for others around us. It was profoundly revolutionary then. It remains in many ways profoundly revolutionary today, particularly in those parts of the world dominated by fierce religious fundamentalism. Undoubtedly we all inhabit a vastly different world because of the experience that Shakyamuni went through at Buddhagaya, and the fire that it lit in him.

But perhaps the most remarkable thing is just how powerfully that experience continues to reach out to us over the vast gap of time; just how astoundingly modern and relevant and life-changing his teaching remains. We find powerful echoes of the most fundamental of Shakyamuni's teaching in so many areas of modern society.

In the Universal Declaration of Human Rights for example, which was created in December 1948, largely as a result of the unbounded horror of the Holocaust, and its utter disregard for the value of a human life. The opening words of the Declaration seek to re-establish the profound truth that the very essence of humanity, what it means indeed to be a human being in the modern world, lies in having respect for the lives and dignity of all other human beings. The Declaration states,

'… recognition of the inherent dignity and of the equal and inalienable rights of all members of the human family is the foundation of freedom, justice and peace in the world.'[2]

That is a sentiment that lies at the very heart of Shakyamuni's message.

As we shall see in more detail in later chapters, we also find powerful echoes of many fundamental Buddhist insights into human motivation and behaviour, in the sort of findings that are coming out of the very latest work by social scientists and psychologists among others, as they seek to define what is it that enables people to feel good about themselves and their lives and their relationships; the kinds of values and behaviour that contribute to a greater sense of stability and resilience and well being, in our hectic, media-filled, time-slicing, modern lives.

We even find echoes in the latest work carried out by the neuroscientists, using MRI scanners to watch the brain at work in real time, that begin to give us a wholly new perspective on human motivation and behaviour.

In fact perhaps the most surprising thing is that there is so profound an accord between the view of human motivation and behaviour presented by Buddhist teachings, that have come to us from many centuries of reflection and analysis and inspiration, and the view that is being constructed for us during the relatively brief period of modern scientific experiment and observation. The extent to which Shakyamuni's insights and perceptions have stood the test of time is truly astounding.

The early spread of Buddhism

After Shakyamuni's death his teachings, which offered a radically new approach to life, and a new kind of hope and optimism available to all men, spread like a bushfire throughout South East Asia. But he also left his followers with a substantial problem, which still has a profound impact on how Buddhism is viewed in the West today. Shakyamuni had taught for several decades, proposing an approach to life that many among his audience must have found difficult to grasp, as he sought to take them with him on a strenuous and wholly novel spiritual journey. Like Jesus many years after him, he taught in the oral tradition, so that none of his words were written down until long after his death. Moreover it was only towards the end of his life that he begin to describe some of his earlier teachings as *provisional,* that is to say, partial or incomplete, a series of way-points if you like, on this stairway to the fuller or more complete understanding expressed in what have become known as his *essential* teachings, the very core of his message.

Any great body of thought tends to get carved up and sliced into by succeeding generations, leading to its being re-interpreted and re-assessed and viewed from widely different perspectives. It is if you like an inevitable aspect of the history of ideas. This undoubtedly happened to the great body of teaching handed down by Shakyamuni, as people sought to interpret exactly what had been handed down to them, and relate it to their lives. The net result is that we end up with a broad spectrum of interpretations and perspectives. Moreover, every great religious or philosophical tradition needs to renew and re-examine itself regularly, if it is to stay meaningful and relevant to people's lives. Buddhism is no exception

But one of the major results as far as Buddhism is concerned is that quite early in its history, a few hundred years after Shakyamuni's death, two great rivers of Buddhist belief and practice had developed, that are most often and most simply described as the Southern and the Northern transmissions.

Theravada Buddhism

The river of belief and practice that flowed south and east into Sri Lanka and Thailand and South East Asia is based largely on the earlier teachings. This Southern Buddhism is known technically as Theravada Buddhism, or the Teaching of the Elders. Occasionally it is called Hinayana Buddhism, although since Hinayana is translated as 'the lesser vehicle,' this term is very much less used today because it clearly carries a somewhat derogatory message. This stream of Buddhist practice and belief has a marked tendency towards conservatism and monasticism, or a full blown religious life. It is marked by immensely detailed codes of observance, often so detailed that only those who are prepared to abandon their ordinary lives, and take up a monastic life have the time to follow them to the letter. It is also renowned in parts of South East Asia for its ornate temples, often with huge, ornate statues of the Shakyamuni, giving him a god-like status. In his book *The Buddha in Daily Life*, Richard Causton has characterised Theravada or Hinayana Buddhism as follows;

"This is probably the form of Buddhism best known in the West; for some it has even created the impression that Buddhism involves the worship of idols. Moreover, since the application of Hinayana Buddhism to daily life is limited, its appeal to date has been mainly as a subject for academic study. This has naturally tended to reinforce the idea…that Buddhism is primarily concerned with intellectual abstraction, a means of escaping from the material side of life into a 'higher reality,' through various forms of physical and mental discipline."[3]

Accepting the fact that there is a very great risk of over simplification in seeking to define the essential character of any great philosophy, this mode of practice might be described as reflecting teachings that were dominant in Shakyamuni's earlier years as a religious leader.

Mahayana Buddhism

However his primary focus was undoubtedly the ordinary daily lives of ordinary people. Those are the people he spoke to in huge numbers as he moved around the country. And this primary focus is strongly reflected in the other great river of Buddhist thought that flowed North and East, through Tibet and China in the early years of the Christian era, and eventually reached Korea and Japan. This is Northern or Mahayana Buddhism as it's most often called. The central teachings of Mahayana Buddhism were formulated at least in part as a reaction to the ascetic and essentially monastic tradition of earlier Buddhism. It places all its emphasis on carrying Buddhist values and principles into the lives of ordinary people living out their lives wholly in the secular world, raising families, coping with all the trials and tribulations that life in the real world presents us with. Indeed the title 'Mahayana' is most often translated as 'the greater vehicle' to make clear its purpose to carry all people, of every way of life and background, towards a higher life state.

This book swims entirely in this northern river.

The Lotus Sutra

A key point to hold onto in this brief potted history is that the central text of Mahayana Buddhism is deemed to be a work known as the Lotus Sutra, which stands alongside other great writings such as the Torah, and the New Testament and the Koran as one of the primary religious works of human history. Sutra simply means text or teaching, while the lotus of the title is seen to be a powerful metaphor for several key ideas. Not least, since it is a plant that grows in muddy, swampy environments, and yet bears the most beautiful flowers, it is symbolic of the immense potential locked up in the mundane travail of human life, which a Buddhist practice seeks to release.

This long, involved and complex text is made up of 28 chapters filled with extraordinary images and parable-like stories. It is not a read for the faint hearted, it doesn't yield its riches easily. But the truths that it tells were the dominant theme of Shakyamuni's mission during the later period of his life, and in this sense it is described as representing the very core and essence of his life's work. It is only in the Lotus Sutra that he expresses his most fundamental insight, namely that what is called Buddhahood, or Buddha nature, is not a quality, or a life state, that is restricted to just one or two or indeed a limited number of especially gifted people in human history. It is, he declares a universal quality, available to all, part of our common humanity, and with effort and commitment and application we can all lay claim to it.

It is Mahayana Buddhism that first attached the word 'nature' to the word Buddha, to express this profound, life changing idea, that this supremely positive, optimistic, compassionate life state is potentially available to all of us. In doing so it profoundly changed the way Buddhism was practised in South East Asia, particularly in China and Japan. Although, as Shakyamuni himself was only too well aware, the message of the Lotus Sutra was by no means an easy one for ordinary people to accept, or believe in, then or now. As he declares in the Lotus Sutra itself;

"Among all the sutras that I have preached, now preach, and will preach, the Lotus Sutra is the most difficult to believe in and the most difficult to understand."[4]

It is thus the Lotus Sutra that lies at the heart of the Mahayana teaching, that we can *train ourselves* in the skills of hope and optimism, that we are not in any way hemmed in or restricted by our circumstances, or indeed by our past, but that we all have the ability to develop this strong and positive inner space, that is resilient and robust enough to carry us through any challenge we might face. That is if you like, the great promise that draws many people today to a Buddhist practice.

Threads in the same piece of cloth

Some people may be troubled or distracted by the fact that there are today a substantial number of different Buddhist schools, although of course, we are quite accustomed to the fact that a kind of fracturing into different groupings is a common feature of all the major world religions. To a greater or lesser extent we find it in Christianity and Judaism and Islam and Hinduism. It would seem almost inevitable that wherever you have a great body of thought that seeks to explain or illuminate for us the immense complexities of life, then it will be subject to different interpretations at different times and in different places. In that sense it is really doing no more than mirror the complexity of the life that it is seeking to illuminate, and should be seen as a richness rather than as a confusion. Rather than detracting from the central message, these different schools and patterns of belief are perhaps more accurately viewed as simply different threads, in what remains very much the same piece of cloth.

But it's important I think to add a coda to the story of Shakyamuni, that brings it up to date, and establishes the direct link between Shakyamuni and the philosophy embodied in the Lotus Sutra, and the rapid growth of Buddhism in today's world.

—⁓—

CHAPTER FIVE

Buddhism in the Modern World

I heard an extremely interesting observation made not so long ago by a senior religious figure. It was made by a Christian Bishop as it happens, as part of an open debate on the role of religion in society. It has stayed with me, and I think it bears centrally on our discussion. He argued that traditionally in the West, people have sought the expression of their deepest spirituality within the established forms of religion. But, he believes that during his career experience, a matter of some 40 years or so, there has been a profound sea change. People in his view haven't lost touch with or rejected their spirituality, although that is the comment that is often made. He argues that most people still seek a vehicle within which they can express their spirituality, but they want it, it seems, without the structure and the rituals of formalised religion. They want that is, the sense of liberation and freedom that comes from experiencing their spirituality directly, in their own person, free from the formalities and time-honoured rituals that are so much a part of the established churches.

That observation represents I think, a genuine insight. It offers perhaps, at least a partial explanation for the fact that, over the past 40 to 50 years, many tens of thousands of people in Europe and the Americas for example, have chosen to adopt a Buddhist practice. For the very first time in its history, Buddhism is flowing strongly westwards, out of Japan and Asia, into Europe and the Americas and elsewhere, possibly because it answers in so many ways to the need that the bishop has observed. Indeed the extraordinary fact is that never before in its history has Buddhism spread so rapidly or so widely in terms of geographical area, and never before in the religious history of the West, have so many people turned to Buddhism to seek their answers to their questions about life, the universe and everything.

There are no easy answers to explain this process. The people who have adopted Buddhism in the West come from all walks of life, all kinds of backgrounds, all kinds of careers. Ordinary people, living in the real world, bringing up families, pursuing their careers, and choosing to put it all together within the framework of a Buddhist set of principles and beliefs. It is a genuine revolution of sorts. Indeed it has been described by religious historians as a 'new departure' in the religious history of the West.

What makes it all the more remarkable perhaps is that this movement is taking place in an age that is far more noteworthy for its rampant materialism and widespread cynicism than its religious commitment, because a Buddhist practice is genuinely demanding. It calls for constant application and effort because you are learning a new set of life skills, fundamentally new ways of thinking about your life, and how to tackle the problems that are inherent in all our lives.

A Buddha called Nichiren

Many Buddhist teachers, both ancient and modern, have had a role to play in this 'new departure.' But strange as it may seem, undoubtedly one of the most influential of them, who has had a major role to play in the evolution and transmission of Buddhist teachings into the modern world, was a great thinker and writer, a Buddha indeed, called Nichiren Daishonin, who lived in 13th Century Japan. We need to look briefly at his life and works. Nichiren Buddhism is one of the most prominent and vibrant threads in that cloth that we call Mahayana Buddhism.

He was born in 1222 in a small fishing village in central Japan. He spent virtually all his life immersed in study and in teaching, and yet in reaching out, in very much the same way as Shakyamuni had done, to ordinary people in every walk of life. The hallmark of his life was his immense courage and compassion in challenging the ruthless military junta or dictatorship that had supreme power in Japan at the time, over its abuse of power and neglect of the welfare of the common people.

Historically speaking, Nichiren, like Shakyamuni before him, was a profound and fearless social reformer. He was born into a rigidly feudal society, ruled over by the powerful military dictatorship, with the support of various sectarian priesthoods who enjoyed immense privilege in high places as a result, and who had a dominant influence over the lives of ordinary people. Women had virtually no rights. Peasant farmers had no status. And yet here was Nichiren, openly preaching a Buddhism of extraordinary modernity, that spoke of the universality of Buddhahood for all, men and women alike, respect for the individual whatever his or her status in society, and the potential for everyone to learn how to create a more fulfilling life for themselves, whatever their circumstances. It was the very stuff of social revolution, and inevitably he became a marked man, feared by the priests of the schools he challenged and defeated in debate, persecuted by the military rulers whose authoritarian approach to government he openly sought to reform.

If one were to cast around in modern history to find a similar figure who sought, virtually alone, to achieve similar profound changes in society in the face of so much resistance, it might be a Ghandi or a Mandela, or perhaps a Martin Luther King.

A message of hope

In strictly religious terms, Nichiren spent his entire life clarifying the essence of Shakyamuni's teachings and helping ordinary people to see their Buddhism as wholly practical, not a thing apart, but very much part of the fabric of their daily lives. He remained close to his followers constantly, supporting and guiding and writing to them through countless everyday problems. Everyday then, and just as everyday now, from anxiety over a sick child, to a dispute with an employer, to ill health, to grief at the death of a partner. The most extraordinary thing perhaps is that the letters still exist. A timeless record of the transforming power of a Buddhist practice for ordinary people, living ordinary daily lives.

Always the message is the positive one of hope and optimism. He is always seeking to deepen their grasp of the profound paradox that lies at the very heart of Buddhism. The understanding that although we instinctively reject and shy away from the troubles of life, it is only in fact by embracing them, or facing up to them and challenging them as they occur, that we can learn how to transform them into the strength and the confidence and the resilience that are the basis of a solid and durable sense of well being. The only school to a better life you might say, is life itself.

He taught that when we are weak, our problems seem huge, even overwhelming. When we are strong however, the problems no longer appear so daunting, or insuperable. The essential issue therefore is not how to eliminate problems from one's life, which is a manifest delusion, since it can never be achieved, but how to grow that inner strength of spirit to overcome them, which is eminently achievable. It's that inner strength that alone enables us to maintain our stability and our optimism and confidence, even when the going gets tough, as of course it's bound to.

A practice for ordinary people

In several ways Nichiren went further than any other Buddhist teacher, before or since. He did two immensely important things. He re-established what had become completely obscured in the proliferation of Buddhist sects over the years, namely the primacy of the Lotus Sutra as the essential bearer of Shakyamuni's teaching, with it's message of the universality of Buddhahood. Then, from the depths of his own experience, and his profound understanding of human nature, he revealed, or created, an immensely simple, down-to-earth, daily practice by means of which ordinary people, living ordinary workaday lives, could begin to grow that inner strength, regardless of the demands pressing in upon them from their daily work. He created a daily discipline if you like, to enable people to train themselves in skills that are immensely valuable in all our lives, resilience and self-reliance and a sense of self worth and confidence in our ability to cope.

That may sound a huge oversimplification, and it is of course. But that in essence was Nichiren's great contribution, creating a model of Buddhist practice that is accessible and available to everyone. Then and now. Wholly accessible to people today for example living busy, active, multi-tasking lives in a modern society. That is one of the reasons no doubt, why he is sometimes called the Buddha for the Modern Age.

When Nichiren Daishonin died at the age of 60, his legacy was simply immense. He could be said to have launched the modern global revolution in Mahayana Buddhism, that continues to spread. He is one of the main reasons why Buddhism remains among the world's fastest growing religions, and why it has begun to flow energetically westwards, out from Japan and Asia, and into the Americas and Europe. He created a teaching and a practice that has the potential not only to transform an individual approach to life, but it has the reach and the capacity, to transform from the bottom up, the way modern societies work.

And yet, for most of us in the West, when we hear the word Buddhism, it means little or nothing to us. We don't have any clear images or markers to hang onto. For Christianity of course, even for complete non-Christians, there are plenty because of the long years during which we have been immersed in a Judao-Christian culture. Whereas the mention of Buddhism summons up for most of us a series of vague stereotypes at best; a vast nebulous, mysterious philosophy with no clear themes or messages, throngs of saffron-robed priests dodging the traffic in Bangkok, ornate temples filled with huge god-like golden statues of the Buddha, and a generalised idea perhaps, that it is largely to do with a withdrawal from the cut and thrust and hurly burly of modern life, into some inner meditative sanctum.

Surely it's time to move on?

If, as the evolutionary biologists and the behavioural scientists tell us, a greater sense of well being at the heart of our lives is fundamentally what we are all seeking, and if as Buddhism claims, it is essentially about increasing the sum total of happiness in a tough and challenging world, then it would seem to make sense to spend some time and energy to dig beneath the stereotypes, to understand more clearly just what it is that Buddhism has to offer.

—∭—

CHAPTER SIX

Buddhism Is Not A Morality

The opening line of Thich Nhat Hanh's remarkable text book, *The Heart of The Buddha's Teaching*, goes as follows,

'Buddha was not a god. He was a human being like you and me, and he suffered just as we do.'[1]

The Buddha is of course Shakyamuni. His message, that we have just been talking about, was based on his life experiences as an ordinary human being. Moreover, as we've seen, he made no claims to divinity or divine inspiration at any time during his lifetime. Indeed were he to be deified in any way by his followers, that would immediately destroy the validity of his central teaching, namely that the life state that he achieved is available to all of us. We can learn that is how to achieve it, in this lifetime.

The reason why I think it's important to make that point so directly, so bluntly you might say, is because it challenges what is a common, and wholly understandable stereotype in the West, about the sort of being Shakyamuni was. As a purely historical figure Shakyamuni clearly occupies a place in western minds alongside the other great founders of religions who came after him, such as Jesus and Mohammed, who did of course repeatedly claim a divine connection. In fact that connection was the very basis of their authority and the religions they founded. They claimed to be in their different ways, the only connection or channel, through which divine purpose could genuinely be known and understood by ordinary people.

Because of this parallel status, if I may put it that way, we are accustomed in the West to attributing to the title, Buddha, if not the unique qualities of divinity, at least something very close to it. That is the perspective that very much colours the general western response to words such as Buddhahood and Buddha nature, and, there is no doubt, that represents one of the biggest obstacles for many people in the West, in getting to grips with what Buddhism is about.

So let's try to remove one or two of what seem to be the most common misconceptions.

Buddhism is atheistic

The starting point for anyone seeking to understand a little more about Buddhism is that it is atheistic or humanistic. That is to say it doesn't have at its heart, or anywhere else for that matter, the unique, all-powerful, creator-god figure that sits at the centre of all the other major world religions, including of course those most prevalent in western societies, Judaism and Christianity, Islam and Hinduism.

There is no clearer way of saying it than that it is a *man-made* religion, although you won't of course find those words in any Buddhist text. The opening line quoted above is the closest we get to it. So essentially, Buddhist teachings represents the wisdom and insights initially of one man,

Shakyamuni himself, immensely extended and developed and clarified down the succeeding centuries by some of the greatest minds in human history. And that wisdom, that profound understanding of the nature of human life and behaviour and motivation, is passed on to all other men and women, on the basis of *equality.* That is a key point that is really extraordinarily difficult to grasp, even for those who practice …on the basis of equality. We are so accustomed in the West to the fact that there is a vast unbridgeable gulf that normally exists between the teacher, the bearer of the message, the Jesus or the Mohammed, and the rest of humankind. That gulf simply does not exist in Buddhism. Shakyamuni makes that clear throughout his teaching. He tells us repeatedly in order that there should be absolutely no doubt, he is simply one of us.

So what is unquestioned is that if you strip away the legends and the mythology that have inevitably accumulated around so large a life, lived so long ago, Shakyamuni and all the historical Buddhas down the years have been ordinary human beings. They were undoubtedly *extraordinary* in terms of the clarity of their vision, and their profound understanding of the reality of human life, and their ability to convey that understanding to others. But apart from that they had feet of clay so to speak, they manifested many of the ordinary human frailties and they had to bear all the trials and tribulations of ordinary men. Indeed they all went out of their way to stress their ordinary humanity.

What is also unquestioned is that this accumulated wisdom about how to learn, about how to create for oneself a better and a happier life, continues to be about the *present* and not the past. It continues to demonstrate its direct immediacy and relevance, despite the vast changes mankind has lived through in every possible area of life, immense, immeasurable changes, but it's clear that they haven't impaired or weakened the relevance of the message. Some of Buddhism's central teachings for example, about how to draw upon our inner resources to increase our awareness of the detail of our lives and relationships, and so overcome many of the negative impulses and responses that we experience, have been taken up and are used on a daily basis by some of today's pre-eminent psychologists.[2] So Buddhism continues to touch and change people's lives around the world, in the West now as well as the East, in increasing numbers. It remains one of the fastest growing of the major global religions.

So what do we mean by Buddhahood?

If we take the trouble to ask why that might be the case, there are of course many threads to the answer, but undoubtedly a central one lies in the quality we have just highlighted, namely the *ordinary everyday humanity* of the creators of this great body of thought. Just as all the great historical Buddhas were ordinary human beings, it follows almost as the night the day, that we, as ordinary human beings too, have within us the potential to grasp and make use of the accumulated wisdom and the insights that have been passed down to us. We all qualify. No one is excluded. We can all set out on the path to master the skills and the qualities that enable us to make the very most of this life, in the here and now.

Because that is such an important idea, and one that is by no means easy to take on board, Buddhism chooses to attach a special name to this potential we all have. It chooses to call it Buddhahood, which is of course a strange word that we don't encounter very much, if at all. And, like all strange things, it has the power to alienate us, or put us off.

There's nothing wrong of course, with being put off, so long as we are aware of *why* that is the case, and don't allow the alienation that the word itself might inspire, to obscure the usefulness and the down-to-earthness of the message that it carries, which could be immensely valuable to us. As indeed it has already proved itself to be for so many people in the West.

But when it comes down to it, it is just a *name.* When we are prepared to invest a bit of time in understanding what it represents, it very rapidly becomes clear that this *potential* is not in any way about an aspiration to some kind of perfection, or other-worldly elevation. Or anything resembling that. At its simplest, it is about learning how to make the most of the qualities that we all possess. And a Nichiren Buddhist practice, again put at its simplest, is really nothing more, nor of course nothing less, than a life-long, daily, personalised training programme to enable us to make the most of those qualities. Not all that different when it comes down to it, from a personal physical fitness programme that many of us carry out at the gym. Only with a Buddhist practice we are talking about developing *spiritual* muscle if you like, and a mental toughness and resilience.

Basically it's about learning completely at our own pace, how to increase our self awareness, or our *mindfulness* as it is sometimes expressed, so that we can more readily recognise, draw out, make use of, the inner resources that we all possess, of hope and optimism and courage and resilience, and similar qualities that we can all certainly make use of, particularly when the going gets tough. That is not saying of course, that Buddhism is only about handling the tough bits of life. Buddhism is about every aspect of our lives. But the fact is that when things are going swimmingly we can all get by with a laugh or a smile. When they get tough, as they are inclined to do in life, we need all the help we can get. Buddhism argues that we can draw out that help from within our own lives.

So, in a nutshell, a Buddhist practice is essentially about *empowering* all of us, enabling us to make a better fist of life. Enabling us to use *all* the resources that we have, spiritual as well as intellectual, to create value in our own lives, and the lives of others. To increase as I've mentioned, the sum total of human happiness. Which is an easy enough thing to say of course, but which takes real commitment and application to achieve. The daily practice helps us to get better at summoning up that application and commitment.

Hopefully that brief explanation should enable us to sweep a fair number of those initial stereotypes out of the way. We now know that Nichiren Buddhism is not about allegiance to an external deity. It's not about giving things up. It's not about trying to be somehow more spiritual than anyone else. Nor is it, most importantly of all, about a laid down code of behaviour, or a morality.

So what do we mean by morality?

This is a key question in our understanding of Nichiren Buddhism, since we are so accustomed to religions coming complete with a clearly laid down morality. That is to say a set of commandments or dogma or rules of behaviour, that basically tell us the way we should live, the rules we should observe, if we are to live what that particular religion defines as the good life.

So Christianity as we know has its clear sets of commandments and instructions. Both Judaism and Islam have very precise codes of behaviour that even embrace details of everyday living such as what you can eat and when. Hinduism, even in the modern world, has its strict caste system, laying down the life-paths that people can or cannot follow. We tend to take it for granted therefore that Buddhism will also have its own set of dogma or rules of behaviour. But remember the Buddhist scholar Edward Conze's clarification we mentioned earlier, that Shakyamuni always presented himself as a guide rather than an authority.[3]

The great social and ethical power of Buddhism lies precisely in the fact that it is not prescriptive, it doesn't seek to tell us what we should or should not do. Instead it seeks to make us much more keenly aware of the *implications* of our actions, good bad and indifferent, and then places *responsibility* for those actions entirely on ourselves. So in sense you could say that Buddhism is observational rather than prescriptive. It sets out to describe for us in some detail what it sees to be the way our lives work, what kinds of thoughts and actions lead to anxiety and suffering, both for ourselves and those whom our life touches. What kinds of behaviour lead to a sense of profound well being and optimism, again, both for ourselves, and those whom our life touches. That is the accumulated understanding or the wisdom if you like, that the body of Buddhist teaching presents to us. That essentially, is what it's all about, the *motives* and the *impulses* that drive human behaviour, and their effect on our sense of well being.

But then essentially it stands back and says, in the light of that understanding, it's *your* life. No one else can live it for you or tell you how to live it. Only *you* can resolve all the varied influences and impulses, opportunities and difficulties that come to bear on you as you travel along that life journey. No one else can do it for you. And so, by the same token, only *you* can be *responsible* for the way in which you resolve those influences. That is the very heart of the issue. Whereas the other major global religions are built essentially around the idea of *codes of behaviour*, describing what is entailed in trying to lead a good life. Buddhism is built around the idea of *personal responsibility.* We alone it says, are the gardeners of our own life garden. We alone are the producers of our own life programme. In every way, it's our deal. The daily Buddhist practice is if you like, *the support programme* that enables us to develop the courage and the wisdom and the compassion to be able to handle that responsibility more effectively.

Thus central to Buddhist belief is this principle that we alone are responsible for the actions we take, or the causes that we make, good bad and indifferent. And in the same way, wholly responsible for the effects that those causes inevitably plant in our lives, like seeds, good bad and indifferent. At some time, in some place, Buddhism teaches, those seeds will bear fruit.

And the notion of causes embraces the whole spectrum of our actions, which includes thoughts and words as well as actual deeds. Our thoughts govern what we say of course, and both thoughts and words have a powerful role to play in what we actually do.

The connection between cause and effect

When Buddhists use the phrase 'Buddhism is reason,' they are in some measure describing a principle that is central to Buddhist belief, and which comes closest perhaps to something resembling a morality. Namely that there is a sense of balance, a sense of a reasonable relationship between what we *do*, and the *effects* that those actions plant in our life. We reap if you like, what we sow. Although it goes without saying that we may only very rarely be able to work out or to perceive the actual connection between the causes that we make, and the effects they generate.

But even to expect that is in a sense to miss the point. We can all see, or we can all point to some experiences in our life, when we made great efforts and achieved what we wanted. Or when we didn't and saw an opportunity slip away. But that is very much the exception rather than the rule. Since Buddhism is wholly concerned with the reality of daily life, it isn't in any way talking about a direct, perceptible, measurable connection between every cause we make and every effect. That would simply be unreal. It is arguing however, that once we take on board this central idea, accepting total responsibility for all the *values* that we hold, and the *choices* that we make, and the *actions* that we take...total responsibility...then we are introducing a wholly new, and powerfully *positive dynamic*, into our lives. A dynamic that can only bring immensely positive results for ourselves and our families and friends and workmates and communities, all the various societies that we all inhabit.

This is undoubtedly one of the toughest and the most influential Buddhist principles to take on board and to live with. You could argue that Nichiren Buddhism is both immensely refreshing in the sense that it does not seek to lay down a code of behaviour we are expected to follow, but at the same time it is immensely challenging in terms of asking us always to accept full personal responsibility for all our actions.

It is of course much easier said than done, particularly when things go badly wrong. But again paradoxically, it is also an approach to life that is full of hope. Once we accept that the *causes* lie within our own life, then immediately, we can understand that so too, do the *remedies* for changing things, or putting things right. We now have control so to speak, of both halves of the equation.

The extraordinary modernity of Buddhist ideas

Buddhism frequently talks about the notion of a fundamental change in the attitudes and the motivations of a single individual having a profound ripple effect, spreading out like the ripples on a pond, to touch and change in some measure the lives of all those with whom that person comes in contact, and beyond, spreading out into society. It is a crucially important idea of course, because it lies at the very heart of the way in which Buddhism has spread and changed societies down the ages, and continues to spread today. Indeed, one of the most surprising things about Buddhism is the extraordinary modernity of its ideas

That might seem at first glance to be a strange claim to make, modernity is not an idea that is often bracketed together with Buddhism. But it is a claim that stands up to quite rigorous scrutiny. The remarkable fact is that there is a very considerable body of modern social research, that would seem to echo or reinforce many absolutely fundamental Buddhist teachings that have been with us for several hundred years. I deal with a number of these pieces of research in later chapters, but since this is one of the central themes of the book, it seems timely to look at a couple of them now, just to anchor the point. Not, I hasten to add, because they can be considered as in any way to be *proving* long-held Buddhist principles, because of course they don't. Not in any way. Buddhism doesn't claim to be scientific in it's approach, nor is it. But then it doesn't need to be. Nor does it need scientific *validation,* if I may put it that way, for the way it clarifies and illuminates so much about human motivation and behaviour. That illumination has in every way stood the test of time. I mention the research only because it seems to me to open up a new and hugely interesting perspective, it shines a wholly different sort of spotlight onto these fundamental issues, and in that sense, I suggest, it greatly enriches and adds to the breadth of our understanding.

Making determinations

So the first piece of research[4] I have in mind is focused on a little thought about, but immensely significant area of our lives, namely our ability to make decisions or determinations in managing our daily lives. Basically this research set out to explore what were the long term effects on people's lives of differences in their ability to make decisions, and to accept responsibility you might say, for the actions that they took at any point in time. What is particularly interesting about this bit of research is that it was truly longtitudinal, that is to say it followed several hundred people as they went about their lives, over many years, several decades in fact, from youth into adulthood and marriage and a working career and so on. So we know that it was about real people living through real life situations, whereas much social science is essentially about quite small groups of volunteer students, being recruited to play various mind games in laboratories.

What the research illustrated was the fact that we all vary immensely, and from a surprisingly early age, in our ability to make decisions and determinations. We are not talking about major life changing decision here, such as getting married say, or starting a family, but just the ordinary everyday business of getting up in the morning and getting on with our lives throughout the day, making a hundred and one choices as we do so. There is, as in all things human, a spectrum of ability, and we all sit somewhere along that spectrum. Some people are very decisive and controlled about what they are doing and where they are going. Others as we know, just drift, in the sense of being carried along very much more by whim and impulse and chance opportunity.

What the research indicated was that those who are naturally of a decisive turn of mind have an important and valuable gift that, whether they realise it or not, has profound effects in just about every area of their lives. Being able to make determinations and focus our resources to achieve them is an immensely life-enhancing process. However, and this is the really interesting bit as far as this discussion is concerned, it also showed that those who sit in less favoured parts of the spectrum, those that is who were pretty poor at making up their minds, or being clear about what they want to achieve from the events in their life, could be shown a way of getting much better at it.

The researchers were able to show for example that if these people could be persuaded or encouraged to make a determination or introduce a structured activity into any particular area of their lives; the *nature* of the area wasn't all that important, it could be almost anything, a regular exercise regime for example, or work with a charity, or a study programme and so on, but the somewhat surprising result was that there were real and measurable spill-over benefits in many other areas of their lives.

It didn't seem to matter what the initial area was in which they made the determination, so long as it involved two things, real *commitment* to make the determination in the first place, and then the *resolution* to stick at it and put it into effect, despite perhaps a certain amount of reluctance or resistance to start off with. But the key point is that the people involved went on to experience genuine benefits in other areas of their lives, even areas as crucial to our happiness as social and marriage relationships and career progression and so on.

The sheer discipline of making the decision and sticking to it seems to act as a sort of catalyst to trigger these spill-over effects in apparently unrelated areas of these people's lives. And as I mentioned earlier, we are talking about real people and real lives here, rather than anything resembling a laboratory set up.

The more detailed the better

Moreover, and I find this aspect particularly interesting because it comes so close to a Buddhist principle, it seems that the more *detailed* the expression of the determination, the greater the spill-over benefits into other life areas. Not just deciding to do a bit of study for example, or exercise, or some other activity once a week, but doing it on a regular scheduled basis. And the greatest benefits seemed to flow for those who took the trouble to actually write down for example a detailed plan of when or where or how the routine or the regime was going to take place. As one researcher expressed it, people who went to the trouble of making when, where and how plans were about three times more likely to achieve their overall goals.[5]

It is crucially important of course not to be tempted to draw too many parallels or inferences from such research. Certainly we shouldn't adopt it as a sort of scientific scaffolding around any particular Buddhist perception. No research as far as I know has ever been carried out, to prove the value of a Buddhist approach to life. But that having been said, there are at least two clear echoes if I put it no more strongly, that a practising Buddhist would immediately recognise in this research.

One is the undoubted value that this research indicates, arises simply from the structure and the discipline and the regularity inherent in a daily Buddhist practice. It takes immense personal commitment and resolution for example to maintain a daily practice, month after month and year after year, and this research would clearly suggest that very considerable benefits should spill over into other areas of the practitioner's life from that daily commitment and resolution.

The second lies in that finding to do with the detail of the determinations. It echoes closely the constant encouragement inherent in a Nichiren Buddhist practice to make determinations and to set goals, the more detailed the better, writing them down indeed, and to focus one's practice and actions towards achieving them.

Buddhism is very much about recognising and making the very most of opportunities to create value, for oneself and others. If we relate the findings emerging from this social research to that basic Buddhist approach, the conclusion seems inescapable that it is not only immensely modern in its outlook, but that it can only bring with it great value, in many areas of the practitioner's life.

The reality of the ripple effect

The second piece of research in some sense follows on from the first, although the two are not in any way formally connected. It too was carried out largely in America, and it is if anything, even more compelling because it describes a completely new insight, that is still only partially understood. What the sociologists seem to have found is that qualities and feelings and even patterns of behaviour in our life, seem to be able to spread naturally and easily through our network of friendships and relationships, rather like the ripples spreading outwards on a pond, without any conscious effort or activity on our part, or even without our being in the slightest aware that such a process is going on. That is to say, we may not set out in any way with the intention of spreading these qualities, which include fundamentally important states of mind such as happiness and sadness, but nevertheless, the spreading goes on.[6]

We may not do anything in particular. We may not necessarily even speak about them, as far as we are aware, or give any other formal expression to them. But still it seems, there is a gradual percolation, if I may call it that, of views and values and behaviours and feelings that goes on through the various social networks of which we are a part. The effect has been well documented and even measured to some extent. What is still unclear is just how it happens, what the mechanism is. Indeed the sociologists carrying out the research make it quite clear that as yet they have no real explanation of the process by which these emotions and attitudes flow from one person to another. But it does seem that we are far more sensitive than we might have thought, to the kinds of values and views that are held by people who share some part of our social network, even, and this is the really surprising finding, even if that is quite a distant part of our social network

We have to be careful of course, as always, in making connections. There are many factors involved in this sort of social research that are only partially understood. But given the journey we are on, looking at happiness, it is indeed fortunate that one of the life states that the scientists have looked at, and mapped in greatest depth, happens to be the percolation of happiness through what they call these informal social networks of people. As one scientist has expressed it.

'Most people will not be surprised that people with more friends are happier, but what really matters is whether those friends are happy.'[7]

Indeed, what is remarkable is just how extensive the research has revealed these emotional networks to be. The scientists argue, for example, that our own life state, in this case happiness, is undoubtedly affected to some extent not just by our *immediate* neighbours or friends, as you might have thought, but in some measure, by the neighbours of our immediate neighbours as well. And not just by our close friends, but the friends of our close friends, and even their friends too! They talk of at least three degrees of separation. People, that is to say, whom you may actually encounter only very rarely, possibly never, or only at second hand, through the accounts of your friends or neighbours or work colleagues, and even if you are unaware that you are receiving these influences in any way.

So the scientists carrying out this research actually borrow a metaphor from medicine, and talk of these qualities, these states of mind being in some way *contagious or infectious*, almost like a virus, as if we can actually *catch* the happiness or the depression, or the optimism or the negativity from other people in a quite widely spread social network. It is an extremely interesting piece of social research that is still on-going.[8]

The Buddhist connection

But again we are faced with the question, what has all this to do with Buddhism and its beliefs? The short answer is that this research seems to mirror so closely a view of human relationships that has long been expressed in Buddhist commentaries. They talk frequently of how a profound change in the beliefs and attitudes of one person can affect those around him or her, spreading just like that series of ripples on a pond, through family and friends and work colleagues and beyond, in some subtle way coming to affect the attitudes and the perceptions of those further off in a wider community. Daisaku Ikeda for example writes powerfully of this ripple effect when he declares,

'A great revolution in a single individual will help achieve a change in the destiny of society, and further, will enable a change in the destiny of humankind.'[9]

So the views that have come from the gradual evolution of Buddhist teachings, and those that have been observed through modern social research, are clearly not a million miles apart. Although, once again, it's important not to draw too many parallels or to seek to impose too close a relationship, since they are not in fact, related in any way. I am suggesting no more than that this piece of research offers us a quite different, and I think, an immensely illuminating perspective, in looking at what is a strong theme in Buddhist teachings, and which rings true in our daily experience, namely just how closely we are connected with people around us. We all know that we are, in our deepest nature, a gregarious animal. We earnestly seek lasting and fulfilling and harmonious relationships at all levels in our lives. When we achieve them at home and at work and in our local communities for example, they immensely reinforce our creative energies. We become freed off so to speak, to pursue objectives and create value in so many other areas of our life. When they breakdown for whatever reason, the effects can be devastating, and, as this research suggests, not just for ourselves. Such a breakdown can send out shock waves into every corner of our social and working life.

Buddhism in society

The research also very strongly reflects the view that although a Buddhist practice is very much an *individual* activity, enabling people to build a strong and resilient inner self, it only becomes *meaningful* as something that is lived in society. That is to say, the daily determination to live as a Buddhist, rather than simply knowing and understanding Buddhist principles, becomes apparent above all, in the way we handle our relationships. And by that I mean the countless relationships and encounters that occur at every level in our lives, from the most fleeting to the most complex, as we move through each day. Buddhism has always argued that they are all equally important in terms of the ripples we are sending out into society. The most important person in your life, you might say, is the one who is standing in front of you at this moment.

This research would now seem to add a further dimension to that view. That the way we treat and respond to all the people we encounter in the course of the day, from partners and work colleagues to ticket sellers and travelling companions, clearly has effects *well beyond* the people we actually encounter, as they in turn carry those effects on into their relationships, and their social networks.

The importance of respect

Let me just add one further thought to round off this discussion, because it is a centrally important one, both in the context of our own sense of self worth and well being, and also, harking back to the very beginning of this chapter, the nature of the responsibility that Buddhism asks us to accept in our relationships with other people. What you might ask, does Buddhism have to tell us about these encounters, to enable us to create the greatest value in our own lives and in our wider communities? The answer that comes back, as loud and clear as a peal of bells, is the notion of respect. Respect. It is in many ways an old fashioned word, in the sense that we are less likely to hear it talked about today than we used to. But the plain fact is, that it is a central and in some ways a dominant pillar of Buddhist thought.

Both Shakyamuni and Nichiren Daishonin had profoundly revolutionary views of the way societies should function, to achieve the greatest value for all. Those views were based essentially on everyone learning how to respect the dignity and the humanity of every other human being with whom they came in contact, whatever the circumstances. It was revolutionary then, in the sense of being an ideal to be lived up to. When it is expressed in these stark terms it is clear to all of us that it remains pretty revolutionary today. But let's be absolutely clear what it is asking us to do, because, I would argue, it is in no way an outlandish or extreme goal, nor one that is beyond our individual abilities. All it asks is that if we want to live in a society that is based fundamentally on respect for the life and the values of each individual, as most of us undoubtedly do, then we have to demonstrate that respect as a core quality in all *our relationships and encounters*. Not some, but all. It doesn't ask us to like everybody, or to admire them, still less to love them, or to take them into our lives. We just have to dig deep into our own better selves, whatever the circumstances, and recognise their common humanity.

That's all. No more, no less.

But it is also the very heart of the matter. If the idea sounds simplistic it does so only because we are all so strongly conditioned by the tides of envy and anger and contempt and competition that can flood through our lives, that the idea of living our lives based on respect just seems somehow afar off. But is it? Hold your judgement for a moment, because it is, I suggest, simply being very practical and down to earth.

Freedom of choice

Buddhism is very much based on freedom of choice, it is not remember a morality that tells us how to behave. We choose. And that extends right across the spectrum of our lives. Thus it argues that the way we experience any relationship is also a matter of choice. Negative or positive, good or bad, happy or sad, it's our choice. It's not something that is done to us, if I may put it that way, no one does it to us, we do it to ourselves. Whether that is, we choose to fasten onto the bits that we don't happen to like, on the annoyances or the irrationalities or inconsistencies in other people's manner or behaviour that happen to irritate us and make the relationship awkward or inconvenient for us. Or…choose to make the *positive* choice, and dig deeper and determine that we are going to create value out of the encounter, whatever the circumstances and whatever our initial reaction to it.

You'll notice that the word choice occupies a central role in that argument and it will occur again and again in this journey, because it is crucial to an understanding of what Buddhism is about, and indeed to any idea of how it defines happiness or well being. There can be no happiness without hope or optimism, and no hope or optimism without freedom of choice. In a sense it takes us back to the pieces of social research we have just been talking about. Making the *determination* to handle these kinds of situations in a positive way, the research suggests, will not only have powerful spill-over effects in many other areas of our life, it will have positive, ripple-effects in the lives and the social networks of all those we encounter.

Buddhism, as we've seen, has long carried a similar powerful message. In fact it is the basic Buddhist approach to all relationships of whatever kind, right across the field of human experience. It is based on that central, life-changing perception by Shakyamuni all those years ago, that every human being without exception, has this profound potential of Buddhahood within their lives. And the purpose of the daily practice established by Nichiren, is in a sense to sharpen our recognition of that potential in ourselves and others. Why on a daily basis? Because the negativity in our lives, never gives up. It gets up with us every morning, and just as the devil often has the best tunes they say, so too our negativity often has the most potent arguments. Talking about happiness necessarily involves tackling this substantial *anti-happiness* dimension in our lives, so that's where we move next.

—⁓—

CHAPTER SEVEN

How to Strangle the Parrot

Not so long ago I gave a talk on Buddhism that was entitled '*How to strangle the parrot.*' That doesn't sound very Buddhist I know, although as it happens it's not entirely outside the Buddhist tradition. There is a famous sutra or talk that was given by Shakyamuni to his followers, that became known as the sutra on '*Knowing the better way to catch a snake.*' In fact it deals with a similar theme, namely how to still the restless movement of the mind during meditation or chanting. The meditator is seeking to still the mind for a while to create a space, to allow other parts of the consciousness to come through. That's the whole purpose of the exercise. Meanwhile the restless ceaseless mind will have none of it and wants to go on drawing up shopping lists or reminding us of pressing appointments, or re-running conversations, or responding to a difficult letter. So focusing on the method of the chanting or meditation exercise to quieten down the mind's restlessness is a skill that we have to learn. And like all new skills, it takes a bit of time to get right.

But back to my parrot. I was using it of course as a metaphor to represent the negativity that we all have as part of our make up. Buddhism teaches that we all have it to some degree, whether we believe or accept that we have it or not, even those of us who are apparently blessed with the sunniest and most positive of temperaments. Indeed Buddhism teaches that we will *always* have it as a fundamental part of our humanity, however positive a spirit we learn how to develop and maintain. As we know from our personal experience, let alone from Buddhist teachings, it is one of our potential life states, always lurking there ready to put in an appearance if we let it. So any parrot strangling that goes on is never strictly terminal!

Psychologists tell us that we talk to ourselves all the time. As a sort constant process of reasoning and rehearsing and working things over in our mind, we hold this constant inner, ruminating conversation with ourselves. It is so much a part of our life that we take this inner whispering voice or voices, very much for granted. And this wretched parrot that I mention is one of those voices. A negative one, a powerful advocate for *not* doing things or not challenging our situation. When I say that it gets up with us every morning, it is because it is so often in the mornings that it is at its most vociferous.

People often say for example, that early mornings are a kind of low point in their day that they have to struggle to dig themselves out of. Many people talk of experiencing such a low point, hence perhaps the global addiction to the regular morning pick-me-up fix of caffeine. But this parrot perches on our shoulder so to speak, throughout the day. Its very considerable power lies in the fact that it knows us *infinitely well.* We have no hiding place. It knows even the slightest and most well concealed chinks in our armour and precisely where we are at our weakest and most vulnerable. So our personal parrot often has the most subtle and insidious and persuasive arguments.

And what it does basically is to go on sniping and whittling away at our self confidence and courage, constantly taking advantage of those half-formed inner stirrings of doubt and fear and uncertainty that we scarcely admit to ourselves. It knows about them. It knows precisely for example, why we won't succeed at this or that endeavour, why we won't get the job, or the promotion, or whatever it is that is currently uppermost in our sights.

When we are strong and confident and on a high, or we've just had a victory, we can often just brush this insidious sniping aside, laugh at it, or ignore it into silence. But when we are at a low ebb, or when we have just had a rejection or when we're really reaching for something that we know is a bit of a stretch, it can often be all that is needed to tip us into a powerfully negative and defeatist frame of mind. And if that pattern is repeated often enough, this time and last time, and the time before that, it can stay with us to become a habitual mind-set.

Life can become, *'there's no point in even trying,'* rather than, *'I really think I can make a go of this.'* Or to paraphrase Barrack Obama's stirring nomination speech, we allow ourselves to retreat from *'yes… we can'* to *'no… we haven't a chance.'*

The parrot is real
And there is no doubt that this parrot exists, and it's important not to underestimate his or her influence. We all have some experience of course of what he means to us in everyday life. We all recognise at once the huge difference that exists between the positive, optimistic, hope-filled person we happen to know at work, who gets things done and encourages and inspires people around them, even when everybody is fully aware of the steepness of the challenge. And the reverse, the powerfully paralysing effect

even a single pessimistic colleague can have, spilling their doubts and their negativity into the workplace as if they were emptying a suitcase.

So the parrot that sits on our shoulder every day, without fail, can have a profound effect not just on our personal lives, but on the lives of those around us. What's all this got to do with Buddhism you might ask? And the short answer is carried in the wonderful Buddhist word of *mindfulness,* or awareness as we might translate it, although I think it loses much in the translation. It is only by being mindful, or aware, of the constant reality of our negativity and its potential influence on our mindset, that we are able to go into battle against it. Indeed it is only with this awareness that we can begin to establish control over the negative functions in our lives.

Who is holding the reins?

There is a well known Buddhist story, once told never forgotten, that gives us a slightly different perspective on the same issue. It tells of a horseman, galloping furiously along the road as if he has an urgent mission to achieve. He seems to know where he is going, and he clearly has to get somewhere in haste in order to get some important job done, because the horse is travelling pell-mell, kicking up the dust as he goes.

So a bystander shouts out to the horseman, '*Where are you off to? What direction are you heading in?*

As he hurtles past the horseman shouts back, '*Don't ask me...ask the horse!*'

Who has control the story is asking? Whose making the choices?

Are we simply being swept along by the relentless tide of events that makes up all our daily lives, and by what is sometimes called our deeply ingrained *habit-energy*. Or do we feel an inner sense of...not exactly control because rarely are we wholly and entirely in control of our lives...but having a clear sense of direction and purpose, and a stability underlying the inevitable daily flux of events. One of the things that struck me most strongly for example when I first started to go to Buddhist discussion meetings and seminars, long before I myself took up the practice in any steady or meaningful way, was that people would very often remark on this as one of the effects of their practice. People would frequently say that they felt more focused somehow, even if they couldn't define precisely why, or that they no longer felt so blown off course by random events, or that they felt they could make choices and decisions more readily, because they had a clearer sense of an objective or a direction.

The decisive power of mindfulness

That is undoubtedly a key point that is worth hanging on to in our thinking about happiness, or establishing a stable sense of well being. To squeeze it absolutely into a nutshell, Buddhism essentially presents the flow of life as a constant series of choices, lying on this continuum between the negative and the positive. It argues that all the time, every hour, every day, every week a thousand times perhaps, we are all called upon to make the choice between being positive and value creating, or being negative and in some measure...great or small...destructive. And what it seeks to do is to bring to us the constant mindfulness, the awareness, that *we are the ones making the choice.* That we have that capability. That life doesn't just *happen* to us, as we commonly view it, we *make it happen.* So we are not just being carried along by our habit-horse, we have some clear sense of holding the reins and directing its progress.

And all Buddhist practice, at its heart, is about that heightened awareness. About helping us to grow and to nurture if you like, rather as we might nurture a plant as a conscious act, the inner courage and the sense of self confidence and the sense of self worth, so that we can more often recognise...recognition is a crucial part of the process... and reject the negative, however persuasive it might be, and more and more often make the positive choice.

And it is that progression, that growth, that enables us to become more capable, more effective, more contributing, in all the multiple roles that we all have to fulfil, as parents and as partners and teachers, as colleagues at work and as friends at play, as people that is living in society. And we might add, given the theme of this book, the most happy. Since our *awareness* of our own improved self confidence, and of our own greatly increased ability to contribute to others, plays a huge role in what constitutes our happiness. We want fundamentally to be capable people, in all the roles that we inhabit.

Buddhism chooses to call that resilient, life-enhancing inner strength that we can learn how to grow, Buddhahood, and it chooses to call the confident awareness of its existence, enlightenment. Those may well be unusual and infrequently used words in our daily vocabulary, but the key point is that the qualities they represent are not to be seen in any way as other-worldly or esoteric qualities. They are essentially everyday. Part of our everyday reality.

As we discussed a moment ago, modern psychological research has revealed just how powerfully the development of those qualities I've just described can affect our environment and the people we come in contact with, in all the areas of our life. Qualities like courage and self confidence and compassion are, as we've seen, immensely contagious in ways that we would not have thought possible. But where this is leading us is towards an idea that is central to our understanding of what we mean when we think about Buddhism in daily life. Because fundamental to the idea of strangling the negative parrot, and controlling the galloping horse, is this principle we have already touched upon to some extent, of accepting personal responsibility for what goes on in our life.

So whose responsible?

On the face of it that doesn't sound very challenging does it? I mean something called Personal Responsibility is scarcely a new or a resounding idea. I think you might even find it in the smaller print perhaps, in the odd political party manifesto, as being a quality that should be fostered, and should even perhaps be folded into the school curriculum. I have to say I think that would be a great initiative. As an idea properly instituted, it undoubtedly has the power to transform society. But it does mean following through all its implications.

What does that mean exactly? Well, I'm sure we all like to think that we are indeed in charge, that we are wholly responsible for everything that we say and do. No question. Of course we are. We always have been. We're very responsible. Except, we might add… after a brief pause…for those instances when clearly *someone else* was responsible, for a fierce argument because they were so unreasonable, or a bitter conflict, or an objective that wasn't achieved, or perhaps a marriage breaking up, or some such thing. We can't be expected to accept responsibility for those kinds of things as well, can we? I mean those things that were, well…clearly someone else's fault?

What Buddhism does if you like, is to lay it clearly on the line. No ifs. No buts. We are responsible it argues, for what goes on in our lives. Period. Even if, as so often happens to all of us, we would *prefer* not to be, and prefer to point the finger at someone else, and exclaim, or shout, or protest, about where the responsibility in this particular case lies. Buddhism says quite clearly, don't look for the causes out there, look for them in here, within one's own life, because that is where they will be.

Once again it is a tough principle to take on board and to live with, on a daily basis that is, with family and friends and work colleagues, because it runs so strongly counter to what comes instinctively. It's not just so much easier, it is immensely *satisfying,* just to give in to the anger, or the frustration, or the intense sense of self righteousness, and to assign the blame elsewhere. To offload it onto someone or something else. Anything to get rid off it. We all do it without a second thought.

Whereas, as we all know, it is both immensely difficult and challenging to calm down, take a deep breath, and force ourselves to look at the situation as objectively as we can. To put ourselves in the other person's shoes if you like, and ask ourselves what were the causes that *we* made, to arrive at what has taken place.

The galloping horse story that we mentioned a moment ago is precisely about doing just that. Slowing down and pausing for thought in order to make a better choice, a more informed or a less heated decision. A slightly more colloquial version of the same idea that came to me from a Buddhist teacher, goes something like,

'anger is very much like cow pats…best handled when cold!'

That may indeed be homespun wisdom, but it is nonetheless wise.

Buddhism in daily life

But there are I think two or three key points that arise from this brief look at our negativity and our personal responsibility for it, that tell us a great deal about the way Buddhism works in daily life, to enhance this sense of being capable, which in turn makes such a big contribution towards our deep seated sense of confidence and well being.

One is that Buddhism requires us, encourages us, helps us, to be clear-eyed and not to fudge the issue. To be clear that is about who we are and what our values are. In this particular case it is of course far easier to blame other people for things that go wrong in our lives, but in fact that approach solves nothing. As we have all experienced, more often than not, it simply serves to prolong the conflict, or the pain and suffering, endlessly. Even though it is infinitely more difficult and challenging to accept responsibility, and look within our own life for the causes of whatever it is that hasn't worked out, it is by a long way the most hope-filled, and the most productive choice. It embodies above all the promise, that if the causes are to be found within, so too are the remedies or the solutions, which means we can immediately do something about putting them into effect.

It also means that once we make the determination to accept the challenge, to accept this crucial idea of our personal responsibility, then every time this kind of situation occurs again, as it's bound to, again and again, it becomes easier to arrive at a resolution. We are putting ourselves in a position to make the positive choice more often, and more readily. We are setting up a win-win situation in our lives.

Moreover it doesn't take long to recognise that we are not talking about huge, earth-shaking changes in attitude. Indeed much of Buddhist teaching is about getting us just to look again at some of the ordinary everyday assumptions that we carry around with us. Brushing away the film of familiarity if you like. Buddhism talks again and again about clarifying our vision, or taking the time to look clearly at our life, so that we get to see with much greater clarity, just how much we take for granted, just how much that is, we have to be thankful for in our lives.

It remains the same old world. It's just that our perception of it is slightly shifted. And that's the key. Everything but everything in our lives is driven by our perceptions, how we think, which in turn governs what we say, and how we act. Even a slight shift in our perceptions will change fundamentally the way we behave, towards ourselves and towards others. And strange as it may seem it may only be a slight change, but time and time again it proves to be enough, to enable us to tackle the problem with a completely different, and infinitely more positive attitude.

And every time it does so, it gives us a little lift inside. A greater sense you might say, of our own capability to resolve problems, and we make a mental note to try to deal with the next issue that comes along in the same personally responsible way. It means that instead of being stuck in a sort of complaining rut, we are much more open to the possibilities in any situation. We open up above all to the possibility of moving on from being generally anxious and negative about problems, to being focused and positive about them.

Of course it's not a one-way street. We're only human, so it can be one step forward, two steps back. Of course. But we're not standing still. We're growing a skill that is not only priceless in the affairs of daily life, but an absolutely huge step along the path that we are following, towards building a happier life for ourselves, and those whom our life touches.

The Story of Claire

In 1984 Claire Bertschinger started working for the Red Cross as a nurse in the war-torn Tigrey province of Ethiopia, where hundreds of thousands of ordinary men, women and children were dying of famine and disease. The disaster was caused by a disastrous combination of circumstances, the extreme drought and famine in the country, the civil war, and an international community that seemed not to want to get involved.

Thousands of people displaced by the fighting converged on the town where she was based. They had walked long distances to where they believed they would be helped and fed, only to find that there was not enough to go round, and they were left starving. The area surrounding the town was a war zone and even travel within it was restricted with checkpoints and armed soldiers.

She felt as if she had been dumped into a kind of hell. In fact it was a feeding centre for just 300 children under 5 years of age. Due to lack of supplies they were unable to feed more than that. But with the combination of severe drought and the civil war, many hundreds of families gathered outside the centre pleading for help for their children.

Claire took the only action that was available to her. She went outside the gates and, walking up and down the lines of people sitting in the dust, tried to select those children who were obviously the most desperately in need. But it was in many ways an impossible task. Everyone there was in desperate need. Claire had to struggle not to make eye contact with the mothers in the lines because that might be seen as a signal for them to throw their children into her arms or to clamour for her closer attention. Entry cards were handed to the children she selected to go into the feeding centre for attention. But as Claire wrote at the time, she felt not a scrap of pleasure at giving out these cards, only deep pain. She felt sick at heart because every card given seemed to represent a sort of god-like power of selection over those who might live and those who might die. She could only hand out about 50 or 60 cards when there were well over 1200 children, all of them starving or sick in some way, little more than skin and bone, crying, or lying still in the dust, covered in sores, overrun with flies, the parents pleading for their children's lives.

Claire's every day was dominated by this desperate struggle to feed as many children as possible… and the death and suffering of so many others. At the time she felt that she was personally responsible for letting them die because she hadn't been able to bring them into the feeding centre. No matter how much justification she might draw from the effects of the war or the terrible drought, ultimately she knew she was there to save lives, and she was clearly failing to do that if thousands were dying. She felt unable to shake of the idea that it was her fault. She was the one not saving their lives, and that was after all, what she was there to do.

Claire had no idea at all what was going on in the outside world, but a BBC news team with reporter Michael Buerk went to Ethiopia to interview her. As a result of their news report a huge fund-raising movement got underway in the UK, driven by the heart-rending footage of the feeding station, the starving, dying children, and the life and death decisions Claire was having to make every day. The news report provoked a tremendous reaction and thousands of pounds poured into charities from people all over the UK. The broadcast was also seen by the musician Bob Geldorf. Recognising the intolerable situation she was in, being vested with the power of life and death, he decided that to stand by and do nothing was in a sense tantamount to murder. He pulled a group of musicians together to record a song entitled 'Feed the World,' which rapidly became the biggest selling record of all time. It raised £8 million pounds and within ten days of the news report aid started to reach Ethiopia.

But isolated in her feeding station in Tigrey, Claire still knew nothing of all this.

A year later she returned to the UK, but she remained deeply affected by her experience. She felt strongly that her family and friends couldn't really grasp anything of what she had been through, or have any idea of just how profound the effect had been on her. So she felt emotionally cut off and isolated, and her own perception of the experience in Ethiopia was widely different from the public one. She felt in fact that that she had been more like a Nazi who had sent people off to the death camps, than the angel of mercy portrayed by the media. In fact she felt that if people realised the dreadful decisions she had been forced to make, rejecting so many sick and suffering children, she could even be seen as something of a war criminal, with crimes to answer for that, at that time, seemed so real and so immediate to her.

Ethiopia was a life-changing experience. Claire felt that she was left with one huge question. Why? What was this suffering all about? What was her life really all about? Over the following years this question stayed with her during her work as a field nurse with the Red Cross, in Lebanon and later Afghanistan. In effect she went on what might be seen as a personal quest, a personal spiritual journey, examining several faiths and philosophies over several years. Eventually she found the practice of Nichiren Buddhism, and the lay Buddhist organisation known as the SGI, which brought her she felt, some answers about her own life, and a clear direction, a way of working for peace and happiness in this life, for both ourselves and others.

As she wrote some time later, Buddhism brought her the realisation that our happiness is entirely our own responsibility. It means learning how to embrace and take full responsibility for everything that we encounter in our lives both the good and the bad. It is that profound realisation that enables us not just to challenge, but to transform and overcome the suffering that inevitably occurs within all our lives. Moreover that inner personal transformation has far wider implications, it enables us to have a positive effect upon our immediate environment and the wider world.

Her new-found Buddhist faith was soon put to a most severe test, when she was asked to return to Ethiopia with the reporter Michael Buerk, to see what real and lasting effect the public outpouring of compassion and the huge fund raising had wrought. Deep down Claire had still not really come to terms with her experience. She still felt ashamed of her part in what had taken place all those years ago. As a result she had no wish to return to Ethiopia. But she felt that as a Buddhist she should go, both to try to confront and transform her suffering, and to create value in some small way. That was her determination at the time, even though she had no idea as to how she might do that.

Going back however proved to be an extremely difficult and painful experience. Being in Ethiopia and being interviewed about the events at the time of the famine, she completely broke down. She was overwhelmed by intensely painful memories, the shame she had experienced, and the smells and the recalled emotions flooded over her. She was filled with doubt as to the possibility of creating value by returning to the scene. She had half expected some kind of revelation or reconciliation through going back, but none had come. She was filled with questions and self-doubt. All she was able to do was to chant passionately to try to establish some peace in her mind.

When she got back to the UK, the vivid memories of the return to Ethiopia and the real suffering she had put herself through stayed with her. But in chanting about it she began to understand something that had eluded her up to that point. She began to realise just how profoundly her deeply buried feelings of guilt had affected her over the intervening years. As she wrote later, she came to realise that whenever she looked back at those events, all she could ever remember was the pain, the terrible choices she had been forced to make in selecting some children to live and some to die.

As she continued to chant about those events she came to realise that it was only by learning to embrace what had happened all those years ago, only by truly facing up to it, would it become possible for her to confront all the fear and guilt that she had locked away deep inside. Those powerfully negative feelings she realised, were completely blocking her ability to express her potential as a human being and to draw upon her profoundly positive Buddha nature.

That realisation was like making a completely new start. With this new perspective emerging as a result of her Buddhist practice, she felt she was freed from fear. She felt able to embrace and cherish the memories of the love and the fun that she had received, and given, in the midst of such a disaster. She knew that she had fought for those children and those families with all her strength. Her compassion had overflowed, and she had done her very best. But those positive memories had been overwhelmed by her belief that people would think she had acted badly in not saving the lives of more children, and for twenty years she had been trying to compensate for this sense of failure. This had shown itself as a deep-seated lack of respect for herself, which meant that she often didn't care for, or look after herself, and she had often reacted to ordinary situations negatively, as a result of this deep, underlying base of self-doubt and self-criticism.

Going back to Ethiopia, re-living the suffering, had in fact acted as a powerful catalyst, enabling Claire to put those past events, however terrible, into a proper perspective, and to change fundamentally her view of herself and the potential that was opened up by her Buddhist practice. From that new beginning she now felt able to create causes based on love and respect for herself, and to relate in a completely different, more positive way to her environment and the circumstances of her life.

Revisiting Ethiopia as a Buddhist also enabled her to see those events in a completely different light. Buddhism teaches the concept of karma, that we have each of us, made the causes for the conditions of our life, and that our present experiences are in that sense, of our own making. This poses the question of course, do the Ethiopians or anyone else suffering in this war-torn, famine-stricken world somehow deserve their plight? The Buddhist answer is very clear. Namely that life, all life, is the most precious of treasures, and thus a disaster, on the scale of Ethiopia, cannot be regarded as solely the responsibility of Ethiopians. It is clearly a *global* tragedy that so many thousands of lives are lost in such painful circumstances. It is part of the karma, the responsibility if you like, of all of us, of the entire world, karma created through the fundamental causes of greed and anger and ignorance. If we work to change these poisons within ourselves, and in the society around us, then we are genuinely working to prevent the circumstances in which such disasters occur.

—⚏—

CHAPTER EIGHT

Buddhism and the Pursuit of Happiness

Few of us I think really know how to value the quality of our lives from moment to moment, although most of us I'm sure, can recognise, in a kind of detached and intellectual way, what a valuable quality that would be to have, since it opens up the possibility of a considerably richer and fuller life. Living in the moment so to speak, rather than just passing through the moment, as most of us tend to do. We often expend far more energy looking forwards, to some special event some time ahead, a holiday perhaps, or a celebration, or a journey to some new place, rather than on what we are experiencing right now, at this moment. But in itself, the *recognition* of the value of living in the now, doesn't actually get us very far. The idea remains somewhat detached, because however desirable it might seem, we're not quite sure how we achieve it, and objectives that we can't see any way of achieving, or where we can't see any path that we might follow towards them, invariably remain out on the periphery of our thought processes.

If we squeeze it down to it's absolute essentials, Buddhism is about learning how to establish just such a path, establishing that kind of awareness of the value of our moment-to-moment daily life. It is one of the most fundamental qualities that in my view sets Buddhism so clearly apart, because it presents itself, right from the start, as being about happiness in this life. Not happiness in some *idealised* life space, or some *vision* of a pleasant life we might hope to achieve, when this or that qualification has been achieved, or this or that obstacle removed. Many of us find ourselves trapped in this prison of the 'when,' as it has been called. Only when this or that change has taken place, then we might be happy.

Buddhism argues that whether we realise it or not, whether we believe it or not, or understand it or not, we have within us all the resources we need to choose happiness in this life, and to establish a stable sense of well being in our lives. And it goes much further, it argues that we can learn how to achieve that goal now. Not just in the good times, but anytime. No matter how challenging and disturbing the circumstances or vicissitudes that we encounter. Not just when the times are golden and uplifting, but when they are resoundingly challenging and down-casting.

That is of course a huge and a life-changing idea, and one that is so unusual, so counter-intuitive, that it is extremely difficult for most of us to accept when we first encounter it. There must be some sort of catch we say to ourselves.

It takes time to learn that there isn't. That the catch is primarily our own lack of conviction in ourselves.

A new life skill

What there is however is the need for a new life-skill, the willingness to look at and embrace a fundamental change of perspective. We need above all to look more keenly at the idea of happiness. Thus, it cannot mean for example, what we so often take for granted that it means, namely the absence of difficulties or challenges. If that were the case it would very rarely occur for anyone, if at all, given that for all of us, difficulties and problems of one kind or another are an absolutely standard part of our daily lives. For all of us, all the time. Whatever our status or position or circumstances in life. We all have something that at the very least is causing us some anxiety, and very often it may well be causing us a great deal of deep pain and suffering.

What it does mean is an awareness…an awareness that steadily grows into a conviction… that we can build within ourselves the stability and resilience to face up to those inevitable challenges, and overcome them rather than being thrown off balance by them. And it does mean learning how to develop that highly desirable quality that we spoke of a moment ago, namely developing an enduring sense of the value of our lives from moment to moment, and the value of the lives of everyone else we encounter.

Why do we find this idea so unusual, so difficult to accept? I mean it's not complicated is it? It's easy enough to see the immense rationality of it. But still we find it so difficult to accept. Why? That is an important question isn't it? Since the answer gives us a profoundly useful insight into how we may set about overcoming the reluctance. There are of course several reasons we might put forward, but two I think stand out.

Our cultural background
One important reason I believe is that the major religions which form the basic cultural background in the West,

Christianity and Judaism particularly, don't have a great deal to say about happiness. Happiness in this life that is, rather than in some heavenly hereafter, which is of course a key differentiator. There is a great deal that they have to say about qualities such as obedience, and duty, and fortitude and stoicism. They are very strong if you like in the general idea of bearing the burden of life, or just getting on with life. But they don't have much to say about happiness. In fact you have to search long and hard to find the word happiness anywhere in the major religious liturgies, in relation to this life of ours on earth.

The second reason I think is that, whether we have an active spiritual life or not, there is a strong underlying sense in the West that happiness is very much a matter of well...basically chance or accident... rather than as a result of any particular *approach or attitude to life*. If you happen to have a generous helping of happiness, then you can thank your lucky stars for it, with the underlying implication that that is pretty much where it comes from! You have either been blessed with a sunny nature, or the gods, whoever they may be, have chosen to smile upon you. And that is pretty much it.

There is a strong cultural tradition in the West that you can build *material* success from a lowly starting position, and there are of course many frequently recounted examples of just that. Rags to riches and all that. We don't however have a similar cultural tradition that applies to this area of well being, that you can *build* for yourself a happy life, whatever your starting circumstances happen to be. It just doesn't exist, other than the fact that the material success is always assumed to contain happiness within it, so to speak. A proposition that we amply demonstrate to be false in Chapter Fifteen.

A bolder vision

Buddhism however, with its essential humanism, and its confirmed belief in the power of the human spirit does present us with just such a promise. It is essentially focussed on the pursuit of happiness, for oneself and others, as the fundamental objective of human life. In this life that is, in the here and now, rather than in that heavenly hereafter. Even as I write that, after many years of Buddhist practice, I am aware of just how remarkable, just how bold and uncompromising a vision of life that is. And all the more remarkable perhaps, in that it is a view of life that was evolved all those centuries ago, and yet it accords very strongly with the views of today's evolutionary biologists and positive psychologists, who define the pursuit of happiness as the ultimate motivational force in life. Ultimate that is in the sense that it doesn't require any further definition, it speaks for itself.

As I've mentioned, if you ask yourself for example what you want from life for yourself or your partner, or your children, or relatives or friends and acquaintances, the answer turns out to be 'a happy and fulfilled life.' And there is a great deal of modern social research to suggest that that is a universal reaction. It cuts across all the boundaries that you can think of, national, and religious and ethnic and status. It's part if you like of the universal human condition. It may initially be expressed in other terms to do with health, or wealth for example, or relationships, or career success, and many others, but then all of those items are only primary objectives in the sense that they *contribute* to your happiness. They are way-stations you might say, on the route. Otherwise you wouldn't want them, either for yourselves or others.

So that gives us a very different perspective doesn't it? It means that it is possible to express this powerful and life-changing idea that Buddhism is presenting to us, an idea that we find so unusual, and so hard to swallow, by saying that Buddhism is doing no more than *recognising* the essential reality of our universal human nature. Doing no more than pointing out to us that this is the most powerful motivator in human life, and that it can be harnessed as an instrument of change, to enable us to lead fuller and richer lives.

That is why perhaps you will often hear Buddhists declare that Buddhism is reason, Buddhism is common sense.

The essential how
But that slightly different perspective only takes us half way. It may open our eyes to the essential reality of the Buddhist promise, but it doesn't tell us much about the essential *how* does it? We would all I'm sure, sign up to the validity of the central idea, but wanting it isn't achieving it. We have to learn how to achieve it. We have to learn how to take the difficult and intractable material out of which all our lives are fashioned and transform it into stuff of well being. Buddhism deals with this issue by talking of our having to go through the essential step of *recognising* in our hearts, that this is a choice we *can make*. That we can actively set about weaving happiness into the stuff of our lives. And the recognition serves the essential purpose of aligning our hopes and our ambitions and our determinations in the same direction.

The unlikely paradox
And that really takes us to yet another unlikely paradox that lies at the very heart of Buddhist teachings, namely that happiness and suffering are not, as we so often think, entirely different and separate experiences, lying at the

extreme and opposite ends of the wide spectrum of human experience. They are Buddhism tells us, closely and intimately interlinked, almost opposite sides of the same coin.

How can that be you might say? It simply doesn't make sense? We are powerfully conditioned to shun suffering. We actively seek happiness. And they clearly lie in quite different directions. Not so argues Buddhism, that is simply an incomplete and partial view. In the sense that if we believe, as we commonly do, that our happiness in this life is directly dependant on our achieving a smooth, untroubled, sunlit existence, free from anxieties and difficulties, then that is clearly a life-strategy doomed to failure, since there is no such place.

None of us knows anybody, not a single person, who lives such a life.

If, on the other hand we genuinely seek to establish a strong and resilient sense of well being at the core of our lives then that can only be found, Buddhism argues, in the very midst of all the problems that life throws at us, *since that is the only place there is.* That is the only reality. They lie therefore, our happiness and our suffering, in precisely the same direction. Indeed Buddhism argues, the more challenging the problems we encounter and overcome, the greater the potential happiness they can release, since they draw out greater inner courage and resilience to challenge and overcome them. We grow to become you might say, our most capable selves, so that there's not a lot left that can come out of the woodwork to scare us.

And although that may sound at first glance to be a sort of sleight of hand, a mere juggling with words, give it a moments thought, and it soon reveals just how clear-eyed and practical a piece of a guidance it is. It is above all, a philosophy built to last since it is constructed out of the *real circumstances* of our lives, as they really are, tough and challenging, rather than as we frequently wish them to be, soft and easy. Buddhism isn't a soft touch, because life isn't a soft touch.

Capability we learn, in the course of our Buddhist practice, is a very important ingredient in the making of this stuff that we call happiness.

Moreover the sense of well being that this strategy promises, is constructed and put together piece by piece, from *within* rather than from without. It comes in fact only from the courage and the determination and the resilience that we develop within. So it's not fragile, it's not ephemeral. In no way is it dependant upon the influence of our life's ever shifting *external* circumstances.

Astounding modernity

It's easy to regard Shakyamuni as a purely historical figure, whose life only really makes sense in a historical context. After all he lived so long ago. But to think in that way essentially misses the whole point, and we should challenge it. It goes without saying that much has changed of course. But we need also to recognise that much hasn't. Despite our vastly increased material prosperity for example, even today there is much pain and suffering and hardship on the streets of our cities, just as he observed in the towns in India all those years ago. And it is present in the West as well as in the East, and in the most extravagantly rich parts of the world as well as the most desperately poor.

And in terms of our individual humanity, the questions he was seeking answers to, about the real nature of the human condition, and the suffering with which it is so closely bound up, undoubtedly remain as valid. What can be done about it? Is it inevitable and unavoidable? Or can people come to a deeper understanding of the nature of their lives, and so create a better, more hopeful way to live? He knew of course that he couldn't transform the physical processes of life. He had to understand more fully the nature and the potential of the human spirit.

The result of that questioning is the body of understanding and teaching that we call Buddhism, and it is vital that we keep in mind the central truth that it is a *practice,* not just an idea. You have to take the action.

Thus if we want a beautiful garden then we know full well that we can't just dream about it, or think it into being. We take it for granted that we have to bend down and get our hands dirty. We have to take a spade and a trowel and we have to dig and heave and lift and move, to work the intractable earth and shape the garden we have in our minds eye, to bring it into existence. Similarly Buddhism argues that if we genuinely seek to establish a durable sense of well being at the centre of our lives, not wishful thinking, but genuine determination, then we can't just think it into existence. Wanting it isn't having it. We have to work at it, by consciously growing and shaping the understanding and the resilience and the courage, and the judgement. All the qualities that we seek to have, and know that we need, if we are to become truly capable people, able to take on anything that life throws at us, no matter how challenging, and overcome it.

Happiness that is to say is not in someone else's gift. It's not something that a parent or a partner or a lover or a child, or for that matter a particular job or a million pounds can give to us, however much we believe that they can or will. We have to make it for ourselves. That is of course a pivotal thought, and it's one we return to again and again.

—⁓—

CHAPTER NINE

A Question of Attitude

No one wants pains and problems. No one wants the anxiety and the tension and the stress that comes from difficulties and problems that emerge in our lives in a seemingly endless stream. So the natural human response is to argue that what we have to do is to get rid of them! We have to arrange our lives in such a way that we eliminate them, or insulate ourselves from them, so that they don't disturb the basic equanimity of our lives. In fact in modern society we allocate huge amounts of time and energy and resources, and not to mention very considerable amounts of money and ingenuity, in trying to do just that, creating a whole variety of these insulating barriers, to keep the rough and tough and anxiety-creating side of life at bay.

Where we aren't completely successful in the insulating business, as we cannot be of course, then we are often complicit in creating a kind of *fiction* that we share with one another. What that means in practice is that although problems and crises and challenges of one kind or another, and the pain and anxiety they bring, continue to absorb a considerable portion of our daily energies, we choose to treat them as a kind of *abnormal intrusion,* into the normal flows and patterns of our life. No matter how regular or indeed how disturbing they are in terms of de-railing the routine of our lives, we seem to have a deeply rooted ability to cling on to the fiction that they are in fact the exception rather than the rule. We persuade ourselves time and time again, that as soon as this particular hiccup, setback, anxiety, disaster, has passed us by, our life will revert to its normal untroubled, non-problematic state.

Why? Because that's the life state we firmly believe we need to be happy, the one without the hassle. In fact you could say that we are addicted to that idea. And when of course that doesn't happen, the fiction doesn't dissipate, or indeed lose any of its strength. We simply extend it to cover the next little crop of troubles.

Both of these strategies have their rightful place of course. They both help. No one would question the prudence of arranging whatever insulation or insurance we can. And though the fiction strategy may not actually deflect the problems, it does seem have a powerful role to play in keeping the deepest anxiety or despair at bay.

Our attitude determines our outcomes

But we're talking about life-time strategies here, that involve all of us, throughout all our lives. So we all share you might say, a deep and common interest in them. This remember is real stuff, this is how we actually *handle* the daily detail of our lives. So perhaps we should ask the key question of whether they actually work, these strategies? Are they adequate? Because there is undoubtedly I think, a powerful downside to them as a basic mindset or approach to life.

For as long as we continue to regard these problems and difficulties as a direct *challenge* to our equanimity and peace of mind, then, by definition, that equanimity and peace of mind will continue to be challenged. In a sense we lock ourselves into a self-perpetuating cycle of cause and effect. We reinforce what you might call a self-conditioning process. So that we can become deeply conditioned pretty much from childhood, watching our parent's reactions and so on, as they respond to difficulties and problems in only one way, and that's negatively. And since problems inevitably continue to occur in all our lives, so does the negative response. In a way it becomes very much like Pavlov's dogs. We carefully forge this more or less unbreakable link in our minds between the occurrence of problems, and the anxiety and stress with which we have always associated them. It becomes so much the way of the world, for ourselves and all those around us, that we never challenge it. We accept it as the sole reality.

Is it conceivable that there might be another reality?

Basically it's a matter of choice

Well, once again Buddhism presents us with an unusual paradox. In fact it stands the usual response on its head. It argues that instead of responding to any kind of problem that occurs negatively and with a measure of anxiety, it is eminently possible to *train ourselves* to see them quite differently. We have persistently trained ourselves to see them negatively. We can just as well, Buddhism argues, train ourselves to see them positively.

The way Buddhism puts it is to say that we need to grasp the immense power that resides in our *freedom of choice.* We can choose how we respond. It's as simple and as life-changing as that. No more, no less.

We have the intellectual and spiritual ability, so, Buddhism argues, we can make the *determination* to see problems and challenges not as an inevitably painful and anxiety-making factor in our lives, but positively as an opportunity. Indeed you could argue, the *only* opportunity we have to grow and develop our resilience and self confidence and optimism and general all-round capability.

Before you throw the book across the room with frustration and disbelief, just stay with the argument for a bit, because it has some way to go. If you think about it, the common response to such a radical idea is bound to be deeply sceptical, but that simply underlines just how deeply conditioned we all are to the negativity and anxiety that problems of just about any kind, big, small or indifferent, generate. We all of course prefer to focus on the sunshine and the happiness in our lives. But as we also know so well, harsh reality has this nasty and persistent habit of intruding.

Indeed Buddhism was in a sense created out of that very same harsh reality, out of the perception that life is tough, and that making our happiness out of that toughness is, so to speak, our deal. We just have to get on with it. So at the very heart of Buddhism we have this fundamental understanding, that how we *choose to respond* to that toughness governs completely, indeed determines, the kind of life that we can build for ourselves.

How we choose to respond, determine our outcomes.

We're all in the same boat

And never perhaps has it been more apparent than in this age of a 24 hour media, driven by a seemingly insatiable desire for gossip and exposure, that this principle goes for all of us, without exception. For those who are celebrated and powerful and wealthy, as well as for those who aren't. It's just the nature of the toughness that's different. We're all immensely conditioned to believe for example that wealth is some kind of *answer*, that it can deliver a more or less complete insurance, a kind of impregnable barrier against the blows of reality that we all seek. But every single day the media circus regales us with stories to prove the lie. Indeed the reverse is true, it's clear that wealth and status bring their own very challenging set of problems. So however much material prosperity may change the superficial circumstances, it may get rid of hunger and cold for example, but it cannot change the fundamental commonality of the human condition. We're all in that sense in the same boat. There's no perfect insulation that we can buy to keep at bay the pains and problems that come with our humanity. So the *external* solutions that we are strongly inclined to pin our hopes on, of wealth and status and success and celebrity don't provide us with an answer. In fact they don't fundamentally alter anything.

Buddhism argues that the only meaningful solution has to come from within. We have to learn a different set of life-building skills. We have to learn that is to look at the pains and problems differently. And as if to prove it's validity, this age old Buddhist principle has become the driving force behind one of the most successful modern methods adopted by psychologists for the treatment of anxiety and depression. As one leading exponent of this method has expressed it, they have learned that they can *transform* a persons experience, just by changing the way that person *views* or pays attention to that experience.

Crisis equals opportunity
Several analogies spring to mind. The Chinese characters that represent the concept of crisis for example, also

represent the concept of opportunity. See the situation as a crisis and it is immediately threatening to the spirit. See it as an opportunity and it is immediately inspiring. The *situation* remains precisely the same, but the attitude towards it is radically different, and the attitude, Buddhism argues, the choice, governs the outcome.

That is the crucial shift in attitude which, Buddhism suggests, it is abundantly possible for us to achieve. The problems remain the same, but our sense of being able to overcome them can change profoundly, and that in turn, means that they are no longer anywhere near so threatening or disturbing. In fact we consciously respond to them in a completely different way. Problems that we believe we can overcome we tend to call *challenges,* and the change of name is by no means superficial. In fact it's immensely influential in its effect on our spirit. Problems are negative and knock us down. Challenges are stimulating and lift us up

It's crucially important to see the clear distinction between this positive response that I have been talking about, and something like stoicism, or putting a brave face on things, which basically means simply putting up with problems for as long as they stick around, and not seeking to change them. As I've mentioned, perhaps because of our fundamentally Judaeo-Christian culture, we happen to have in the West a very strong tradition of qualities such as duty and obedience and stoicism and so on. We are very good at being broad shouldered, and putting up with problems for as long as they stick around.

Being positive about problems is radically different. It is essentially about seeking to *transform* the situation not just to endure it; to create value out of difficulty, to transform potential anxiety into a more consistent sense of well being for oneself, and for all those involved in the situation.

A personal training programme

So Buddhism isn't in any way about a form of *escapism,* about finding some inner meditative refuge from the pace and clamour and constant complexity of modern life. Although that happens to be a very common stereotype of what Buddhism is about, getting away from it all, at least for a time. Buddhism is above all about challenge, about challenging attitudes and behaviours that don't lead us to a positive outcome. It's far easier of course to go on loathing problems that arise and responding to them instinctively, and that means negatively. Few things in life can be more difficult than challenging patterns of thought and behaviour that we have spent years cultivating and nurturing and embedding into our lives. Those patterns of thought and behaviour *are us.* That's who we are. And changing who we are is indeed a tough challenge.

But setting out to achieve that change is, essentially, the role that the daily Buddhist practice plays. In a sense you can think of it as a life- time training programme aimed at changing those negative patterns of thought and behaviour. The objective is to build for ourselves a sense of optimism and self confidence and well-being, that is strong enough and deeply-rooted enough not to be dismantled or blown away by all the difficulties and problems and the emotional and material crises that we all experience. That's the attitude change we are seeking. And we can't simply *think* our way into it, any more than we can think ourselves thin, or think ourselves strong, despite what so many books on the self-help shelves of the local bookshop promise.

We have to take the *action* so to speak. We have to learn what amounts to a new life-skill, in very much the same way, and with pretty much the same sort of determination and commitment as the athlete or the sportsman has to put in, if they want to improve reflexes and embed new skills, in order to get the best out of their body.

Practical and down to earth

So although Buddhism, as with all other religions, has a strongly mystical dimension, you can think about a Buddhist practice in a purely practical, matter-of-fact way. Buddhists *train hard* you might say, to develop more positive, more optimistic, more resilient patterns of thought and behaviour. And like most training programmes, it's a continuous process, with highs and lows, and with many digressions and even regressions on the way. By no means is it all progress. In my experience it will not be what you are told, or indeed what you read that will determine whether or not a Buddhist practice makes sense in terms of your own life, although of course they have an immensely important role, particularly at the outset. In the end it has to be the gradual accumulation of *your own positive experiences* that convince you of its validity.

The plain fact is that however good a teacher we might encounter, we simply can't be *taught* by someone to be positive and optimistic in the face of life's troubles. We have to *learn* it for ourselves, and we can only do that… by doing it.

So the central and somewhat surprising Buddhist proposition is that problems and difficulties provide the pathway, the essential means, the opportunity if you like, for what you might think of as a spiritual work-out, a spiritual training programme. In fact Buddhism goes further than that, it argues that it is the *only* work out available. There is no other. Just as the only place to develop your skills as a swimmer are in the water, or your skills as a tennis player are on the court, so Buddhism argues, the only place to develop your ability to challenge and overcome life's problems and difficulties, with a positive and optimistic and hopeful spirit, is life itself, in the very midst of those problems and difficulties themselves. There is no other place to develop the spiritual muscle that you need.

Nobody said it would be easy

Nobody would suggest that that is an easy lesson to take on board, or to put in practice. It is a real challenge. It requires in a sense a complete re-shaping of our natural response to life's difficulties. Buddhism in that sense, is full of powerful paradoxes. But that having been said, as soon as you begin to think more deeply about what is involved, it clearly makes sense.

It's not just that there are many physical parallels we can call upon to illustrate the validity of the argument. We take it absolutely for granted for example, that top sportsmen and athletes are prepared to summon up all their energies, to push themselves through a pain barrier, in training session after training session, to inch themselves up the fitness and performance ladder towards their full potential. Indeed they would argue that they would be completely letting themselves down if they didn't. They emerge *on the other side so speak,* not just fitter and more capable athletes, but immensely happier, as a result of their own personal sense of achievement. We are all familiar with the sheer vitality and energy and joy expressed on an athlete's face when they know that they have pushed themselves to a new personal best.

Attitude training, Buddhism argues, has a similar energy-releasing, life-enhancing quality, and if we think about it for a moment, we all have some experience of that.

Our personal experience

We all know for example, that whenever we succeed in achieving some difficult goal or objective that we have really set our sights on, something that we really want, we all feel an immense lift of the spirit. We complete a particularly difficult assignment on time say, or we get appointed to a job against tough competition, or we play a major role in helping a friend or a colleague overcome a really challenging situation in their lives, and each time the victory gives a powerful boost to our personal sense of confidence and capability. We feel altogether stronger. And the greater the hurdle we have overcome, the greater the boost. For some time we experience a much greater confidence in our ability to deal with things in general, not just in that particular sphere, but right across the spectrum of our lives and activities. And with that increased confidence and capability comes an increased sense of well being. For a period we enjoy if you like a considerably higher life state.

Buddhism argues that since we know that this potential is there in our lives, it is undoubtedly possible to build on it and extend it. If we can do it once, we can do it twice, and many times. We can take that is, a fleeting and occasional experience, and make it a regular experience. We clearly can't achieve great victories every day of our lives, since the opportunities don't present themselves that frequently, but we can achieve small victories. And the inherent sense of well being can become a daily experience, because of the energy and the optimism and the confidence that is generated by the daily practice.

The discipline of the daily Buddhist practice is of course crucial. It takes us in a sense back to the social research we talked about earlier in Chapter Six, where the introduction of a regular structure into our lives, a structure that clearly involves a combination of determination and resolution in carrying it through, has been shown to create benefits that spill over into all the other areas of our lives.

Immensely Liberating

So a teaching that might at first seem strange, not to say unreal, has the potential to be immensely powerful and liberating. It shows how it is possible to face up to difficult, even impossible situations, and not simply to endure or survive them, but to turn them round completely, and create confidence and value and a sense of achievement out of crisis.

What is clear therefore, in this wholly natural quest for happiness, a key factor is knowing *where to look*. If we have a fixed idea in our mind, a blueprint so to speak, of what constitutes our happiness, then that can often be the biggest single obstacle to our achieving it. If we continue to hang on to the idea for example, that we can only really establish peace of mind and sense of well being in the absence of problems, then that is simply running away from reality.

As one Buddhist text puts it,,

'Don't run away. Touch your suffering and embrace it.'

That is such a simple statement but it has immense potency. Embrace it. All that is saying basically is 'get real!' If we genuinely seek a strong durable sense of stability and well being at the core of our lives then it argues, that can *only* be built in the very midst of the many trials and tribulations that we encounter, by developing the wisdom and the courage to embrace them and transform them. That is of course swift and easy to say, difficult to achieve. The purpose of the daily Buddhist practice is precisely to help us grow that wisdom and that courage.

But what it reveals to us ultimately is that whether we realise it or not, whether we yet believe it or not, there is a profound truth in the understanding that lies at the heart of Buddhism, that our sense of well being in this life, far from being a matter of chance or accident or plain good fortune, as we so often believe it to be, comes down to a matter of choice. Our choice. And Buddhism teaches that we can all learn how to make that choice. It's an idea that has the power to change all our lives if we are prepared to test it out.

—◊◊—

CHAPTER TEN

A Brief Excursion into the Brain

The brain is both a marvel and a mystery. It is undoubtedly the most remarkable item in the entire universe, and even when we are involved in the most mundane of tasks, catching a ball, running up the stairs, riding a push bike, our brain carries out miracles of complexity every single second. The mystery is quite how it is capable of such continuous, unremitting complexity, most of which we are completely unaware of. Indeed what is utterly surprising is that the more we learn about the brain, the more it seems, we discover just how small a proportion of the whole, is the bit we are actually consciously aware of. One neuroscientist recently described the conscious bit of the brain as a sort of humble bookkeeper, keeping track of what has gone on, and laying down a sketchy plan for what we are about to do, but an infinitely small operation, compared with all the stuff that is going on in what we call the unconscious, or sub conscious part of our brain. It seems that in that sense the conscious bit is indeed relatively limited, in terms of the number of issues it can handle at any one time, and in what one might call, it's thought processing speeds.

As it happens, that chimes completely with the view expressed by the late philosopher-historian Arnold Toynbee, when he writes,

'Consciousness is merely the manifest surface of the psyche. It is like the visible tip of the iceberg, the bulk of which is submerged.'[1]

The iceberg of course floats with only about 10% of its bulk above water. As it happens that view expressed some years ago is now widely supported by the findings emerging in several different fields of neuroscience. It seems clear that the subconscious has a much bigger role than was generally believed to be the case in the higher mental faculties that really define the unique qualities of human life, the qualities we value so highly, the complexities of our language, the boundless scope of our spiritual life, the immense range of our abilities to imagine and to think in abstract terms that have led to the vast richness of art and philosophy and science in our lives. Toynbee goes on to add an interesting observation on what might be called the history of man's exploration of the conscious and sub conscious aspects of the brain.

'The discovery of the sub-conscious depths of the psyche, which started in the West only as recently as Freud's generation was anticipated in India at least as early as the generation of the Buddha (Shakyamuni) and his Hindu contemporaries, that is to say at least 2400 years before Freud...Westerners have much to learn in this field from Indian and East Asian experience.'[2]

That basic proposition, that the conscious part of our brain, the part that we wake up with so to speak and consciously use to navigate ourselves through the thousand and one bits of business that make up our day, is really only the tip of the iceberg, opens up the intriguing possibility of the sheer richness and scope of perception we might we able to release, if we could only find a way of harnessing some of the power of the bit that is hidden from us, that we call the subconscious. As it happens of course a Buddhist practice in its various forms, is offered to us as just such a mechanism for enabling us to tap into the power of the subconscious *in some measure*... it's important to bear that qualification in mind...and so make use of it in our daily lives.

And it's worth adding that some of the latest research, some of it only a few months old as I write, seems to confirm just how much the brain seems to have a powerful life of its own so to speak, of which researchers were completely unaware, until quite recently. How did that radical idea emerge? Well, the brain burns up huge amounts of energy, much more pound for pound than any other organ when it is vigorously on line, when we are using it to navigate through traffic for example, or sit an exam, or handle a conversation, or solve a sudoku puzzle. But what took researchers completely by surprise was the discovery that when we consciously choose to switch off, and just snooze or daydream, or otherwise become a couch potato, the brain clearly doesn't. Instead of the brain going into neutral, to conform with our current level of activity, it just keeps going. It seems somehow to switch its manifold circuits to *doing its own thing,* entirely of its own accord, and well below the level of anything we are aware of. The researchers only became aware of it because they discovered that the brain continues to burn just as much energy when it's off-line as far as we are concerned, as when we are consciously working it very hard.[3]

And when the neuroscientists try to theorise, or guess, what is going on, the kind of answers they come up with are that it must be carrying on a kind of essential internal brain admin. So it would be sorting and filing, or creating the narrative story and the memory resource that we may well call upon when we go back on-line. But whatever it's doing, it is a remarkable new glimpse into what you might call…well, the secret life of the brain. And it underlines the fact of just how much we have yet to discover about this remarkable lump of grey matter that sits at the centre of our life.

But what's the point?

But given its apparent complexity, you might ask, do we really need to look at the brain at all on this journey of ours? Will it add to our understanding or just confuse us? I think we need to have at least a brief excursion into this territory, for two main reasons. The first is that the brain of course is where happiness happens. Indeed we know now pretty much where happiness sits you might say. It's not in the heart as the pop ballads continue to tell us, nor in the stomach as the Elizabethans used to have it, it sits more or less directly behind the left eyebrow in what's called the left prefrontal cortex. That is precisely the bit of the brain that is most active when we say we are pleased or happy or content with life. It is also, it's worth adding, part of the last area of our brain to have developed in our long evolutionary journey. The last bit to be added on to complete our emergence as *homo sapiens sapiens*. But we can now definitely say that happiness is not just a feeling, a free floating emotion, as we commonly hold it to be. It has a locus, a home, a sound physiological base.

Indeed when immensely experienced Tibetan Buddhists agreed to meditate as part of a series of experiments with the leading neuroscientist Richard Davidson at the University of Wisconsin, this was the area of their brain that showed intense activity as their meditation progressed. So their meditation generated *subjective* feelings of profound well being and compassion, and this was manifested in the remarkable strength of the activity going on in that particular part of the brain behind the left eyebrow. And it's an important point to hold onto I think, that happiness does indeed have this physiological solid ground if I may express it in that way. It's not just an ephemeral emotion. It's real. It shows up as a real something, in the signals our brain is generating. I ought to add that as part of the same piece of research, ordinary college students, given a brief course on meditation techniques, were able to generate activity in that same happiness area of the brain, although to nowhere near the same extent.[4]

A different kind of relationship

Every action, every experience we have in some way of course derives from the brain. Putting marmalade on the toast at breakfast. Giving up our seat to someone more needy on the train. Experiencing the deep sense of renewal that comes from an hour's chanting or meditation. In some measure, all our thoughts and words and deeds are rooted in and derive from the brain. And if you think about it even briefly the brain demands from us a quite different kind of relationship.

What can I possibly mean by that?

Well most of the other parts of the body show, by their shape or structure, or location, what they do and how they work. A joint is clearly a joint. The heart is clearly a pump. The lungs are clearly air sacs pumping air in and out. The brain however is set quite apart, encased within the thick protective skull, so it can't be directly observed while it's at work, no moving parts, no joints, no valves. And if we ask ourselves which part of our body we most identify our sense of self with, the answer invariably is with somewhere inside our heads. That is to say *I have* a heart and a liver and arms and legs, whereas *I am* in some sense my brain. That is, as I've said, a fundamentally different relationship, and it calls up of course the whole mind-versus-body debate triggered by the 17th century French mathematician and philosopher Descartes, when he famously declared, '*Cogito ergo sum,*' '*I think therefore I am.*'

So that's the first point, I *am* in some sense my brain. The second is that over the past five, possibly ten years, we have learned so much more about what has always been a source of the deepest mystery, namely how the brain actually functions as we think and feel and imagine and respond. And the new knowledge can now add a whole new series of insights into how we think about and understand ourselves, both acting as individuals and relating to our environment. So that some excursion into this territory, however brief, has become it seems to me an inevitable part of any modern journey towards an understanding of the nature of human happiness.

We live in the Age of the Brain

The brain has been studied for centuries. It's known for example that the ancient Egyptians carried out quite complex kinds of brain surgery. Mummies have been found with little holes cut into the skull through which the surgery was carried out. But for many decades our knowledge and understanding of the way the brain functions and its relationship to behaviour, have been based essentially on disability and on serendipity, or pure chance. Someone happens to suffer an accident to the head, or a stroke for example, and the damage to a particular part of the brain has been correlated with particular effects in behaviour, such as loss of speech, or loss of control of particular parts of the body. And very much in that semi-accidental way, slowly and painstakingly over many many decades, a profile has been built up of the various patterns of brain function, with the emphasis being very much on the 'slowly.'

Suddenly all that has changed. In just a few years the whole process has been transformed and immensely accelerated, by the development of powerful techniques such as magnetic resonance imaging machines, or functional MRI scanners as they are known. These machines enable the brain to be studied, for the very first time, in *real* time, as it's actually at work, thinking thoughts and controlling actions. When you lie inside one of these machines it chunters away, a bit like a noisy diesel generator. But for the neuroscientist it's like having a revolutionary new microscope that enables them to look through the thick skull and into the brain directly, and watch the changes in brain activity for example, when a person is thinking about love, or about hate, and many more complex processes than those.

That is clearly a remarkable new threshold. In fact it has led to this time we are living through being dubbed the *Age of the Brain,* because of the torrent of new knowledge, not only about how our brain works, but the implications that new knowledge has for our understanding of the way we behave and respond to those around us and to our environment.

So we are in a sense entering a new era. It is as if quite suddenly, a whole new window has been opened up, through which we are privileged to peer, and learn a host of new things about human behaviour. And that's my main interest in this chapter. That is to say, it is essentially practical rather than theoretical. What new insights can we gain from this sort of research that help us understand more about ourselves, and why we respond in the ways we do. About the way we learn for example, and how we handle anger, and the fundamental roots of empathy and altruism and so on?

I'm interested in two themes in particular, both of which I believe can add something to an understanding of ourselves, and by implication, a Buddhist practice. One is the relationship between mind and body, which has gone through something of a revolution in the West, in recent years. The second is the extent to which the brain is malleable or trainable, which is also an area in which there has been a whole host of new insights in the past decade or so.

But before we get into those particular areas, there are some immensely interesting general insights that come to us from what you might call the basic structural analysis of the brain. Let me just briefly mention one or two that seem to me to be particularly interesting, in the context of course of the journey we happen to be on, trying to understand the roots of human happiness.

The same but different
In terms of shape and size and general layout, all our brains are very similar. They weigh about 1300 to 1400 grams, which makes it immensely large for our body size, around three times as large as the brains of our nearest primate cousins. We have around 100 billion neurons or nerve cells, which are the primary cells of the brain and the nervous system, along which the electrical signals travel. And we have well over 100 trillion connections, or synapses as they are called, where the neurons are interconnected.

The neuroscientists tell us that[5] it is in this intricate network of connections, *the wiring diagram* so to speak, that the power of the brain resides. Herein lies the key to who we uniquely are. Because the wiring diagram is *vastly different* for each one of us, since it reflects all that has happened to us as unique individuals in our lives, all our values, all our preferences, all our multi-layered memories. It is well established that these nerve cells don't die and get renewed like most of the other cells in other parts of the body, nor do they multiply. They remain pretty much the ones we are born with. That means that the vast majority of the nerve cells in our brain today, have been with us all our life. They are us so to speak. It is argued that this is at least one of the reasons for the fact that whatever happens to us on the outside, we feel ourselves to be pretty much the same being on the inside, whatever stage of life we may be at, whether we are 17 or 57.

Old dogs and new tricks

For many decades the conventional wisdom has been that once we became mature adults, our brains were pretty much fixed in terms of form and function. Yes they can change marginally, but the basic wiring diagram so to speak, was thought to be firmly established and fixed in place. That has been the established orthodox view. More recent research however has completely transformed that understanding and turned it on its head. It is now understood that pretty much throughout life the adult brain retains very considerable powers of flexibility, or neuro-plasticity as this quality is called by the neuroscientists.

That is of course a huge new understanding, and it opens up a wonderful new horizon. It means that we retain tremendous possibilities in the extent to which we can *retrain* our brain throughout our lives.

So the implications for all of us, of this long lasting neural flexibility, that we now know we all possess are clearly profound. One for example is that we now know that you *can* teach an old dog to learn new tricks. The old adage is plain wrong. I'm sure many older people have chosen not to take up new learning challenges, not because they weren't capable, but essentially because they were conditioned by the common stereotype that older brains can't hack it, they were frightened off you might say. Another implication is that there is a genuine, use-it-or-lose-it dimension to our brain's alertness and activity. Just as, if we don't use a particular muscle in the body it becomes flabby and weak and loses the ability to function. So, we now know, if we don't actively use the immense flexibility of the brain, the ability to use it, or particular bits of it, diminishes.[6]

Changing attitudes

But what is remarkable is that it is now known that how we *think* can fundamentally change that wiring diagram. That may at first hearing sound strange, since it's the brain that's doing the thinking. One way out of that conundrum I suppose would be to say that the *mind* can change the brain! But leaping nimbly across the bottomless philosophical pit the mere expression of that idea opens up, it has been shown conclusively that *mental* training and discipline, the new *interests* that we take up, the new *choices* that we learn to make, the new *values* and *attitudes* that we adopt, can have a most profound effect on both the structure and the strength of the connections between crucial, life-shaping, areas of the brain.

That clearly has immense resonance with for example, taking up the daily training programme that we happen to call a Buddhist practice, which is concerned essentially with changing our attitudes or the way we approach the ever-changing circumstances of our daily life. As we've seen, Buddhism teaches that although we cannot of course change the fundamental *nature* of life; water you might say is always wet, not sometimes wet, but always wet, that is its very nature, so too, the nature of life is that it is *always* difficult and challenging. But Buddhism constantly encourages us with the idea that we can learn how to change, radically and profoundly, our *attitude* to that life. And so, Buddhism teaches, it is that subtle shift in attitude that enables us to learn how we can transform negative thoughts and emotions and responses, to positive ones. The psychologist Daniel Goleman presents a very similar view in his ground-breaking book *Emotional Intelligence;*

'Optimism and hope- like helplessness and despair- can be learned. Underlying both is an outlook psychologists call self efficacy, the belief that one has mastery over the events of one's life and can meet challenges as they come up. Developing a competency of any kind strengthens the sense of self efficacy.'[7]

One could argue I think that a Buddhist practice is entirely about life-competency, about building an altogether more capable individual.

Handling our emotions

Understandably enough we don't think a great deal about how our brain is made up, we take it all very much for granted, but elsewhere in the same book Goleman goes on to illustrate very interestingly just how crucial a role our emotions and feelings, or you might say our *life state* at any given moment, has to play in all our decision making processes, as a direct result of the basic architecture of the brain, the way the brain that we now have has evolved over the millennia.

He identifies three main stages in the evolution of our brain, stages that are in a sense replayed every time a human embryo develops in the womb. Stage one or the earliest part of our brain to evolve is known as the *brain stem* surrounding the top of the spinal cord. We share this part with all species that have more than a minimal nervous system so it is often called the reptilian brain, since it is indeed shared with reptiles. This bit of our brain isn't involved in thinking or learning processes. It is very much an automatic regulator, monitoring and controlling our basic life support systems such as breathing and body metabolism and a number of stereotypical movements and reactions.

From that most primitive beginning, with the arrival of the first mammals new structures grew up around the brain stem. They're called the *limbic structure* because they're formed roughly in the shape of a ring (limbus is the Latin for a ring) and for the first time they introduced a whole range of emotional responses into the brain's capability. Today when we are experiencing emotions such as fear or longing or despair or anger, it is the limbic system that is involved. But the key point to note perhaps is, there was an emotional brain long before there was a wholly rational thinking one.

And as it evolved this part of the brain developed two crucial and closely interlinked capabilities, memory, remembering past events, and as a result of that remembering, the ability to *learn* from past events. These utterly revolutionary developments gave the animals that possessed them, our distant distant ancestors, a huge evolutionary advantage since they were no longer limited to an automatic range of responses. They could now learn and constantly adapt their responses to changing demands and environments

And finally there was the immense leap forward in intellectual capability that came with the sudden rapid growth of the upper part of the brain, the neocortex as it's called. This is the great lobe of convoluted tissues that grew out of the emotional centres to make up the expansive top layers of the brain. The *homo sapiens* neocortex is so much larger than that of any other related species and it brings with it everything that is uniquely human. The neocortex is the thinking brain, the seat of thought. It enables us to compile and comprehend what the senses tell us of the world about us. It brings the capacity for complex patterns of language and the power of abstract thought and mathematics and philosophy and all the triumphs of art and culture. Above all it has brought the capacity to plan and to adapt and to overcome and surmount all the difficulties and problems that have challenged the human species throughout its history.

But as Goleman makes clear, however powerful a device our rational thinking brain is, it is important to remember that the ancient basic emotional brain continues to play a key role in the way we function today as human beings. Since the bulbous neocortex actually *grew out of* the basic limbic structures they are both intimately intertwined through an infinite number of neural connections. This gives the emotional centres immense power to influence the functioning of the rest of the brain. How we feel at any point in time, what our state of life is from moment to moment, plays a key role in how we think and what we do. We all have some experience of that of course, when we are emotionally disturbed for example we often say so accurately, *'I can't think straight.'* And we have all experienced times when our emotional state or our life state completely overwhelms our ability to function rationally.

Emotional trip wire

As a common example of this facet of our human nature neuroscientists often point to a part of the ancient limbic structures that happens to be called the amygdala. It has been described as a kind of emotional sentinel or trip wire that had an absolutely crucial role to play in our distant ancestor's survival. It receives signals from the senses, from the eye or the ear for example and if those signals contain anything that resembles a threat to life say, or a promise of prey or food, then the amygdala has the power to hijack the brain so to speak, to take it over, to stimulate an *instant* response to flee, or to attack or to chase, while the thinking brain is still going through the multi-layered process of assessing the situation and deciding what to do, using precious milliseconds that might mean loss of life, or loss of the next meal. So the amygdala is the seat of the instant flight or fight response, the sudden outburst of anger, the flood of tears, the flaring spurt of panic.

And it's important for us to know that we have no control over it. When we ask ourselves afterwards, *'Where did all that come from?'* we can be sure that it is the instinctive amygdala that has been at work.

What is absolutely fascinating I think is the fact is that the nerve cells in this part of the brain become 'wired' together when we are young, when we are infants in fact, even before we have language to put our thoughts or our emotions into words, in response to the experience and sensory stimulation we receive at that time. And although this system continues of course to function throughout our life, it doesn't *mature,* it doesn't grow up so to speak. Its responses to the sensory stimuli it receives remain the same, even as we get older. Which accounts for the fact that, as one neuroscientist has expressed it,

'when our emotional 'buttons' are pushed, we retain the ability to react to incoming stimulation as though we were a two year old, even when we are adults.'[8]

We retain the ability that is, however old we are, to throw a completely spontaneous and uncontrolled two-year-old style tantrum or a fit of temper…as we all know to our cost. We never it seems, outgrow it, no matter how mature we get in years. However, it is the experience we steadily build up in the outer layers of the cerebral cortex as we grow older, that enables us to filter out, or modulate, as some neuroscientists describe it, these automatic and instinctive emotional reactions to situations and events, and make the choice to respond in a more measured and mature way. We all continue to have the experience of completely losing our rag from time to time of course, we're only human! But most of the time as adults, although we continue to feel the anger or the fear, we can learn how to moderate our response to achieve a more constructive result.

Once again I think, simply knowing about this basic, life-long connection between two structures in the brain can give us a new and valuable insight. We can see just a fraction more clearly if you like what's going on. And it can help us to see the clear connection between the nature of the mental training that a Buddhist practice offers, and the achievement of a more stable, more compassionate, less reactionary emotional life, which is undoubtedly a big and important aspect of well being.

Two views of time

And one final immensely intriguing insight to do with the way we perceive time, which of course is such a crucial factor in all our lives. The brain as we know is structured in two halves, the left and right hemispheres, connected by a substantial bridge of nerve cells which is called the corpus callosum, (again, just a name). In general its true to say that each hemisphere controls the opposite side of the body, so virtually everyone who is right handed is generally said to be left hemisphere dominant, and vice versa. Although in fact the separation is nowhere near so precise as is generally thought to be the case. About 60% of left-handed people for example are also, left hemisphere dominant.

The two halves work as a single unit. But what modern neuroscience has revealed is the remarkable difference between what goes on in the two hemispheres, in terms of the view of the world that they deliver to us. And perhaps, being aware of just a fraction of it, helps us to appreciate the sheer richness of our inheritance. We are given if you like, two complementary views of what is going on, that are woven together into a single seamless perception of the world.

The right hemisphere we now know, is wholly concerned with the *now.* No time exists for it other than *this present moment*, and each of those moments is rich with detail fed in by our senses. What this precise moment looks like and smells like and sounds like. How we feel about it and experience it. It is the right brain that gives us the ability to remember tiny individual moments in the past as if they were indeed a single snapshot, a particular look perhaps, or a kiss, or moment of acute embarrassment, with the very sharpest clarity, as if it had happened just a moment ago.

It also gives us our capacity to explore, in the single flash of an instant, all the myriad possibilities locked up in each moment. So the right brain is the kingdom of the now.

In contrast the left brain it seems is completely different. It is the kingdom of the *past present and future*. What it does is to take each of those detailed snap-shot moments observed in the right hemisphere and it methodically strings them together like a row of beads. The effect is to constantly put together our life narrative, and to constantly up date it, so that it ties us in with what has just happened to us, and links forward to what is about to happen to us.

So it is the left hemisphere that helps us to do things in the right order, socks always go on before shoes so to speak, not afterwards. It carefully places this precise and present moment into the continuing story that is delivered by the right hemisphere to create the longer, wider, deeper narrative of who we are, where we have been and where we are going, what our life story is.

The inner voice
Interestingly enough, it is also the left hemisphere, the *now* hemisphere, that is also said to be the seat of the inner voice, that we touched upon earlier, that chatters away to us all the time. It is not always of course at the same volume, or at the same level of intensity, it depends on what's going on at the moment. It may remain in the background, or it may on occasion be up close and centre stage. But, the psychologists tell us, it does go on more or less without cease, except when we are asleep, talking to us inconsequentially about what we happen to be doing at the moment, what we've forgotten to do, or what we must do before it's too late. And talking to us historically, in the sense of reminding us all the time who we

are, and what our identity is, what we do, and what people think about us.

Since it is talking to us literally all the time, that inner voice is clearly not simply a bit player in the narrative of our lives. Indeed recent research in the UK and elsewhere has served to emphasise the view that this inner voice not only helps us to think and to perceive the world, it actually has impact on how we *experience* what is going on in our lives from moment to moment. As one article has expressed it;

'…it seems this inner voice changes the way we experience the world.'[9]

This would suggest that it can undoubtedly have a profound effect not simply on our current life state, but on our ability to achieve our goals, and enjoy a sense of well being. If we have a low life state because of a recent failure or a rejection, or because we feel overwhelmed by the current crop of life's problems, so that the inner voice is persistently pessimistic and negative, the effect on our energy levels and our sense of self worth and motivation can clearly be disastrous. If on the other hand that inner voice is more often than not, optimistic and positive it can, just as clearly, lift us up and stir us on to achieve more than we might have thought possible.

Buddhism as we've seen, is essentially about seeking greater happiness in our lives by developing a mental resilience, and a richer and more consistent sense of gratitude for all the on-going aspects of our life. Or we might now put it another way…you could say it's about developing a strong and consistent sense of hope and optimism… in that inner voice.

—∿—

CHAPTER ELEVEN

The Mystery of Mind

This is quite a tough chapter. Indeed I hadn't intended to explore this particularly difficult bit of the mental terrain, when I set out on this journey, until I found myself writing that phrase in the previous chapter, '*One way out of the conundrum I suppose would be to suggest that the mind can change the brain.*' I ought to add immediately perhaps, that that is not a wholly original thought. It, or something very close to it, occurs in a number of papers and commentaries in this very active field of study. But as I wrote it I realised then that it might help just to visit, albeit briefly, the sort of debate on this issue that is going at the moment. I happen to find it immensely interesting. But there are some leading thinkers, including for example, the great American philosopher Daniel Dennet, who choose to argue that there isn't really any issue to discuss here, the mind and the brain are one and the same he argues, consciousness is no more nor no less than the brain at work.

But the title of this chapter is accurate. It is just about the greatest mystery facing neuroscientists, indeed facing all of us, understanding where the brain stops and mind begins. Or to put it in a slightly more rigorous way, understanding how it is that all the hectic, unceasing, electro-chemical activity of the brain, which can be observed and studied by neuroscientists on a purely physical or physiological level, as the movement of atoms and molecules from cell to cell in the brain, because that is precisely how the brain goes about its work… how does that generate an intense sense of self. How does that purely electro-chemical activity become transformed into a sense of someone I call me, living at the centre of a world rich with feelings and emotions and technicolour personal experiences?

The short answer is that nobody really knows. There are lots of theories and lots of debate, and indeed lots of guesses, but nobody knows. Many neuroscientists argue that we might never know. It is such a difficult problem to unravel, with so many unmapped areas, that it is officially labelled by neuroscientists and philosophers as 'The Hard Problem,' with capital letters, to indicate a) that it's a proper noun, and b) that it is indeed properly difficult!

If it's so hard for these expert neuroscientists, you might ask, why on earth should we ordinary mortals bother our brains about it? There are many possible responses, but perhaps one stands out above all, and that is that we all use these terms, the mind and the brain all the time, often interchangeably. Buddhism for example often talks of seeking to be the master of one's mind rather than the mind being master of oneself? Which clearly begs the question, who am I if I am not my mind? So to interpret or to make sense of that statement we have to recognise that it can't really be talking about the *mind* at all, but about something akin to *will or desire.*

So it seems to me it might deliver just a little bit more clarification, a little bit more insight, if we have the courage to take up the challenge, and explore, however briefly, the kind of debate that is swirling around this issue. We may not come up with any answers. In fact I feel sure we won't. But that doesn't really matter does it? If the exploration itself in some way enriches our general understanding, or just enables us to glimpse something new about the extraordinary nature of so much about our lives that we take absolutely for granted, then it's worth it.

There can be no doubt that the mind-brain connection is a truly staggering product of evolutionary development. For all of us, this sense of self, call it mind, call it consciousness, is life itself. It is us. We know we have a lump of matter called the brain inside our skulls, but the mind we feel is something *extra,* something added on. A sort of subtle controller, located we're not quite sure where, but probably somewhere behind the eyes, who uses the material machinery of the brain as part of all the bodily equipment it has available, as we might use a blackberry, or a lap top for example, to help achieve whatever we want to achieve.

In fact neuroscientists tell us that we all tend to think in this way, that we feel strongly that there is somehow a separate and very special bit of us, above and beyond the mere physical and physiological stuff inside our skull. The key question of course is where is it to be found? And as you might expect, in an area of research that is relatively speaking new, and which is so complex, there is a wide range of scientific views.

They are one and the same?

Science tends to work in an essentially reductionist way. That is to say it slices problems down to their smallest component parts, in order to understand each separate bit, and then works out how those bits fit together. So at one extreme we have what we might call the ultimate reductionist view. This argues basically that there is no separation, there is no difference between mind and brain, that they are one and the same thing. According to this view everything that we experience as self, all our joys and griefs, all our intimate and personal thoughts and sensations, all our unique sufferings and our triumphs, can be reduced eventually to being *no more than* the basic electro-chemical activity in the brain; electrical signals flowing along the neurons, chemical transmitters flowing across the synapses or connections between the neurons. This view is now widely held among neuroscientists, and it is sometimes described as removing the *ghost* from the machine, or taking the *soul* out of our humanity, as a way of trying to pin down the effect that this approach has on our perception of ourselves. That is not soul in the strictly Christian sense of course, but soul as a synonym for spirit.

The sort of evidence the neuroscientists bring to bear for this view is powerful, as well as being undeniably fascinating. For example, scientists and neurosurgeons appear to be able to create what we would regard as a personal consciousness, simply by electrically stimulating the brain during surgery. Some brain surgery is carried out with the patient fully conscious, and surgeons have found time and time again, that nothing other than this wholly physical, electrical stimulus, if I may express it that way, of parts of the brain, can summon up what seem to be the most intimate and personal experiences and emotions for the patient, as he's lying there awake in the operating theatre. Experiences that are indistinguishable from what you might call the experience of self, of consciousness. Tiny, uniquely personal moments such as cutting flowers in a summer garden, or playing on the swings as a child, or listening to a mother humming a tune, or holding a loved one's hand at a particular moment.

If a simple electrical stimulus of brain matter can create these virtual moments, that we have come to label as the experience of consciousness, then consciousness they argue, can be no more than the *stuff* the brain is made of. The physical and the material, however complex, is all there is. There's nothing extra, lurking somehow in the gaps between the cells and the molecules, however much we might wish there to be.

That having been said however, it is noteworthy that the late Francis Crick, famously Nobel Laureate for his role in the discovery of the genetic code DNA before he became a neuroscientist, has used the phrase, '*the astonishing hypothesis.*' to describe this ultra materialist point of view, because he finds it so difficult to believe that consciousness is no more than the on-going activity of the brain. And it's worth adding perhaps, that this extreme reductionist view is most commonly expressed in a fractionally more conservative form, as there being no *evidence* for the mind being separate from the brain. Which is not quite the same thing as saying that cannot conceivably be the case.[1]

Beyond our capacity?

Meanwhile at the other extreme there is the view that this exploration is in a sense, a step too far, that our brains simply haven't evolved to unravel the complexity of this mystery. We don't have the capacity to handle it. So, according to this view, just as we know for sure that the brains of all other animals have clear limitations, there are things they cannot do, so too does ours. Our brains, the argument goes, have evolved brilliantly to cope with getting us around, so that we can live successfully in the widest range of habitats of just about any primary animal that has ever lived on earth. They have evolved brilliantly to enable us to mate and reproduce more successfully than any other major animal on earth. They have evolved sufficiently to enable us to work out complex issues such as just how we have evolved the way we have. And they have even evolved sufficiently to enable us to work out precisely where we live in the vast untracked spaces of the Universe.

But unravelling the mystery of mind is, so to speak, a stretch too far. We just don't have the capacity to understand how it is, that the electro-chemical activity in my brain, observed by scientists from the outside, as being nothing more than that, generates this powerful sense of *me* as a thinking feeling individual on the inside. That remains beyond our reach.

Our shared humanity

Wherever one chooses to sit along the extended continuum that links those two extremes, the essential point is undeniable, namely that we all *share* in the astonishing richness of this mind-brain connection. And that is the crucially important point isn't it? It means nothing less than that our actual experience of consciousness lies at the very heart of our *common humanity*. We know in our deepest being that this capacity to experience the furthest reaches of joy and suffering is what we *share* with all the other members of the human race without exception.

As psychologist Daniel Goleman expresses it, it is our shared human consciousness, our inner awareness you might say or our ability to read and comprehend our own sensitivities and emotions and reactions, that fundamentally shapes and moulds the way we relate towards others. The more aware we are, or the better we are at reading *our own* minds, the more closely we can empathise with and relate to other human beings. Empathy as he puts it, is the very root of altruism;

'There is growing evidence that fundamental ethical stances in life stem from underlying emotional capacities. For one, impulse is the medium of emotion; the seed of all impulse is a feeling bursting to express itself in action. Those who are at the mercy of impulse…who lack self control… suffer a moral deficiency. The ability to control impulse is the base of will and character. By the same token the root of altruism lies in empathy, the ability to read emotions in others; lacking a sense of another's need or despair, there is no caring. And if there are two moral stances that our times call for, they are precisely these, self restraint and compassion.' [2]

And Steven Pinker, Professor of Psychology at Harvard writing in a similar vein, passionately extends the range of our conscious connections;

'Once we realise that our own consciousness is a product of our brains, and that other people have brains like ours, a denial of other people's sentience becomes ludicrous. 'Hath not a Jew eyes?' asked Shylock. Today the question is more pointed. Hath not a Jew, or an Arab, or an African, or a baby, or a dog, a cerebral cortex and a thalamus? The undeniable fact that we are all made of the same neural flesh makes it impossible to deny our common capacity to suffer.' [3]

That view so powerfully expressed by a leading neuroscientist, has immense resonance I believe, with the all-embracing Buddhist view of reality, that everything but everything in existence, is interconnected and interdependent at the most profound level. That we are intimately connected not just with all other human beings, but with everything in our environment, and it is in that sense that we play a role in shaping that environment in so many ways that are by no means entirely accessible or apparent to us on a purely *intellectual* level, or dare I say it, on a purely *scientific* level.

Consciousness must include our environment

As it happens there is one increasingly influential school of thought among some neuroscientists that would seem to be completely in rhythm with that fundamental Buddhist view, so let me touch upon it briefly because it is fascinating stuff.

Most discussion about what constitutes mind and consciousness focuses closely on what's going on inside our skulls, or inside our neural systems. With very good reason you might say, since that's where the mind must sit, if it exists at all, inside our heads. There is a new and alternative view however, which proposes that in any discussion of what actually constitutes our consciousness, we have to take the debate *outside* the narrow confines of our head, to include in some measure the physical and social environment in which our head is operating.

In fact it is an idea that is now respectable enough in scientific circles to have gained a title, it's called the *extended mind theory*. It argues basically that the division between mind and environment is much less rigid than was previously thought, and that the mind uses…that's the surprising verb that is applied in this case…the mind uses information from the environment as an extension of itself.

To say the least, that is not an easy idea to grasp is it? In fact at first glance it seems to be a completely outlandish idea. But hang on to your judgement for a moment, because there is a clear rational for it, and it goes something like this. Very little that we experience in our consciousness can be *wholly internal*. And if you think about it for a moment, it can't be. What goes on in our minds necessarily involves a connection of some kind between a *brain event,* if I may put it that way…a signal set buzzing among a cluster of neurons…and some thing or someone in the *outside world* that played a part in triggering the impulse. Because that is the only way, isn't it, that our consciousness can build up a picture of the reality we inhabit?

One simple example that is often given involves a flower. For us to understand in our consciousness the concept of a flower, and to be able to distinguish between a flower, and a stone or a tree or a house say, we must at some stage have come in contact with a real flower, so that this crucial event occurred between something *inside* our heads and something *outside.* And whenever after that we think about or talk about flowers or look at pictures of flowers, we are to some extent referring back to that initial inside-outside connection, or a host of inside-outside connections. Our mind or consciousness if you like, has been altered by that particular connection with our environment.

As the philosopher Raymond Tallis puts it boldly in his book, *The Kingdom of Infinite Space,*

'*The bottom line is this, the brain is a necessary condition of all forms of consciousness, from the slightest twinge of sensation, to the most exquisitely constructed sense of self. It is not however a sufficient condition. Selves are not cooked up, or stored, in brains, or in bits of our brains. ..Selves require bodies as well as brains, material environments as well as bodies, and societies as well as material environments.'⁴*

Another philosopher, Anthony Grayling writes in similar vein,

'The notion that thought is thus essentially connected to the outside world is intended to illustrate the more general idea that mind is not describable in terms of brain activity alone. Instead it must be understood as a relationship between that activity and the external social and physical environment.'⁵

What I find utterly extraordinary, is that in reading a simple primer seeking to explain the basic teachings that Shakyamuni set out all those years ago, you can encounter almost exactly the same pattern of thought then, as the neuroscientist and philosopher expound today. Don't ask me how that can be, but it is. You get a very similar example, and precisely the same conclusion, that our consciousness *cannot and does not exist in a vacuum*, so to speak, solely inside our heads. Its very existence is dependent upon a constant process of interaction with our environment. Here is a brief passage for example, from a brilliant book by a Buddhist teacher,

' …But how can we see our consciousness in a flower? The flower is our consciousness. It is the object of our perception. It is our perception. To perceive means to perceive something. Perception means the coming into existence of the perceiver and the perceived. The flower that we are looking at is part of our consciousness.'⁶

I'm not suggesting that this is an easy thought to absorb over a cup of breakfast coffee. It isn't. But we are much the stronger I would suggest for trying to come to grips with it; to observe the extraordinary fact of scientist and Buddhist teacher using similar language and the same metaphor in their attempts to help us come to a better and richer understanding of a most elusive and complex idea. Namely, an understanding of what it is that enables us to live most meaningfully in this wonderful world we all inhabit.

You can't force the mind

There is one other extremely interesting issue that has arisen as a result of recent research by several groups of psychologists that we ought to mention, since it not only sheds some new and interesting light on the way the mind works, it also reveals the deep wisdom inherent in the Buddhist approach to dealing with anxiety and stress and negativity.[7]

The psychologists talk about this new understanding in various ways. Some say the mind seems to have a mind of its own. Others that you can't force the mind. What they are alluding to in both cases is the fact that if you are beset with negative feelings or anxieties about any particular on-going situation, you can't just *tell* your mind to stop thinking about it. Because it won't. In fact the reverse seems to happen. The more you *tell* your mind to let go of any particular worry, to drop it at once and not give it another thought, the more fiercely it hangs on to it, and amplifies it, and turns it over and looks at it from every possible angle and makes up forecasts about it. The more energy we put into trying to *force* it to let go of this nagging thought, the more energy the mind puts into focusing on it. When we try really hard to tear our mind away to think about something more positive and less anxiety-making, we may succeed for a brief while, but in no time at all we find the nagging thought back in control, even if we have no recollection of how it slipped back in under our mental defences.

Hence the immense and practical wisdom that is now seen to be locked up in the Buddhist practices that seek to transform negative thoughts into positive ones, not by *forcing* the mind away, but by *focusing it* on something else. The psychological research has shown that by *allowing* the mind to focus on a mantra say or a mandala, it serves to steady the mind and calm it down, reducing it's tendency to wander off to think of other things, or go on charging round the racetrack created by its anxious thoughts.

Thus in Nichiren Buddhism we can see the powerful focusing role of the Gohonzon, (see Appendix B) allowing the negative thoughts or impulses to slip away, to be replaced by positive ones. Indeed you will often hear Nichiren Buddhists say that as they chant to the Gohonzon, so their anxieties or their despair seems to slip away, and, as if from nowhere, comes hope.

Have we strayed somewhat from the path of understanding more clearly what we mean, when we talk about human happiness? I have to admit that we have. But not I think without some profit. The rational for dipping albeit briefly into this tricky world of the mind and the brain is essentially to strip away some of the fog of familiarity that masks all this from us. Our mind is so swift and so quicksilver and so self assured in it's handling of all the familiar stuff of our daily lives that we take all this for granted. We never think about it. Stripping away some of the familiarity is the first step in asking us to think about these sorts of issues in a fresh and hopefully, re-invigorated way. As I said at the beginning of this passage, for each of us consciousness is life itself. It's as well perhaps, to understand something about it!

—ᴡᴡ—

CHAPTER TWELVE

Mind and Body

Health is obviously a crucially important dimension of well being. Modern research tells us that in no way is the health we experience simply a physical or a bodily thing, even if it seems to manifest itself in that way. It has a very great deal to do with how we *feel,* the emotional life state if you like, that we tend to inhabit. That's what this chapter is about.

When Descartes made his famous declaration, '*I think therefore I am,*' he set in motion a debate that has continued almost unchecked to this day in one form or another. It's a debate that turns on the issue of the relationship between the mind and the body, or the mind-body dualism as it is most commonly described. The received wisdom until relatively recently in the West has been that they are in a sense separate entities. Locked up in the same body clearly, but essentially separate in terms of the way they operate. After all we can see the body in all its aspects, but we can't see the mind in any shape or form. And as western philosophers have struggled to explain to us for centuries, the world of the body does on the face of it seem to be very different from the world of the mind. The body is above all tangible and it occupies a clearly defined space. The mind is neither, the psychic space inside our heads is not just intangible, it seems to posses the quality of being both infinite and unbounded. It can take us anywhere at any time, and it can summon up towering and intricate structures of the imagination and fantasy from absolutely nothing.

The culture of separation

Moreover this sense of separateness is an idea deeply embedded in the western psyche and in western culture; that the mind in some way *inhabits* the body, and peers out at the world from the control room somewhere behind the eyes like some little space pilot. And whether we are wholly conscious of it or not, we are all to some extent captives of this cultural and spiritual tradition. Indeed the tradition goes further, in the sense that the mind and body are often presented as being not simply separate, but to some extent in *conflict* with each another. This is particularly true in many religious traditions of course, where the mind has long been portrayed as the essentially godly part of us, looking upwards, reflecting our highest mental and spiritual aspirations. Whereas the body is heavily bound to earth, the animal part of us, weighed down by its burden of animal instincts and earthly desires.

Hence the well-documented historical excesses of many of the major religions, in seeking to *intervene* in this presumed conflict, always of course on the side of the spirit. The Inquisition for example, deliberately acting out it's violent executions, believing that only the elimination of the corrupt bodies of its victims by burning them at the stake, would allow their troubled spirits to fly free. And Puritanism, seeking to save souls by banning rowdy physical pleasures such as dancing and funfairs and football, lest they corrupt the dignity and purity of the fragile spirit. Of course those measures, or most of them anyway, are buried far away in the past. But that shouldn't fool us into thinking that the basic idea itself has lost its hold on our perceptions. The tradition is a long one and deeply-rooted, and many elements of it remain. In some parts of the world, in India for example, extreme acts of asceticism are still commonplace, where the body has to be punished almost to the point of extinction, to allow the spirit to progress towards something called enlightenment. While in the West periodic fasting is still commonly practised, and even something as simple as giving up some physical pleasure for Lent such as eating chocolate or drinking wine, is a clear relic of the past, a *symbolic* physical punishment you might say that is seen in some way to ease or lighten the path of the spirit.

Two but not two

The point I really want to make however is that as a result of this long cultural tradition which persists in various guises into the modern era, not least in much of modern medicine, it may well be something of a struggle for us to accept the profound simplicity of the idea that lies right at the very heart of a Buddhist view of a healthy and happy life. Namely the understanding that there is really no meaningful distinction to be made between the *physical* and the *spiritual* aspects of our life. Buddhism uses the beautiful clarity of the phrase '*two but not two*' to encompass this relationship. That is to say the mind and the body may appear superficially to be different entities, yet they are as intimately and as closely connected as the two sides of a sheet of paper, or as your face and its image in the mirror. If you move one, however marginally, you move the other. Whatever affects one will inevitably and immediately affect the other. And not by any means at a superficial level, but right down to the basic life support systems. Right down to the life-changing idea that is central to a Buddhist practice, that suffering and happiness come from *within* rather than without, so that we have the power to choose which we experience. And right down to the understanding that pre-eminent in our own healing processes is our own *life force.*

The modern revolution

In the past, indeed until surprisingly recently in modern times, doctors and scientists have tended to debunk that idea as pretty much mystical smoke and mirrors. But the fact is that right at the cutting edge of modern medical and mind-body research, there is a strongly growing realisation not merely of the *link* between the one and the other, but of just how *closely intertwined* mind and body are. Indeed that the well being of one is intimately involved with the well being of the other in almost every detail. More and more doctors and medical scientists are recognising in their research and in their treatment patterns that how *we feel,* our state of mind, what we are experiencing inwardly, can have the most powerful negative or positive effects on how our body functions. In some cases it seems the mental state can be the *determining* power in how our body functions.

On the negative side the powerful effects of the mind-body relationship are perhaps seen most clearly in links between mental states such as depression and a range of life-diminishing illnesses. Dr. Dwight Evans, Professor of Psychiatry and Medicine and Neuroscience at the University of Pennsylvania, is one among many who has written at length on the intimate link between a mental state such as depression and critical illnesses such as heart disease and cancer and diabetes.[1]

Meanwhile on the positive side a whole host of researchers have written about the immensely life-enhancing and even the life-extending effects of a positive and optimistic mental state. One recent study among many for example comes from an American sociologist, Neal Krause,[2] from the University of Michigan, whose work focuses on stress and the resources people use to cope with it, particularly among the elderly. He has carried out a long term study of some 1500 people extending over a whole decade. He was seeking to establish what kinds of effects there might be on the average health of these people, deriving from a generally high and optimistic life state *related to some religious belief.* And he has certainly identified some extraordinary beneficial effects. In looking for example at how people cope with the kinds of mental and physical stresses that are always associated with a severe economic downturn, he found that people whose life state is based on *altruism,* on giving rather than taking, seem to fare even better in overall health terms than those who are on the receiving end of their compassion or altruism. That is a finding that happens to chime beautifully with a statement once made by the Dalai Lama, that when he gives, the person who receives the gift clearly benefits to some extent, but it is *he himself* he argues, the giver, who receives by far the greatest benefit.

Neal Krause also found that people who are able to maintain a sense of *gratitude* for what's going right in their lives, rather than expending their energies in anxiety over what happens to be going wrong, have a markedly reduced incidence of depression, which is itself held to be a good predictor of general health. He was even able to show that people who continue to set goals and objectives for themselves that are bigger and wider than the simple daily progression of their lives, seem to live not just more happily but for considerably longer. Making sure we continue to have things we *want to achieve* if you like, is truly life enhancing.

All that is in very close agreement with the considerable body of published research that seems to indicate that *a religious belief* of one form or another is seriously good for one's health and length of life. As I mentioned briefly earlier, Dr. Herbert Benson for example, Professor of Medicine at Harvard, conducted a long series of studies into the effect on health of various forms of prayer and religious belief and his conclusion is unequivocal. Namely that many forms of prayer based on belief, undoubtedly have powerful beneficial effects on absolutely critical bodily factors such as lower blood pressure, a stable heart rate and a more effective immune system.[3]

The power of optimism

It's important to be clear I think just how illuminating that statement is. It is declaring that a purely *mental* process such as prayer, used on a regular basis and crucially linked to an underlying system of belief, has been shown to help people recover from their *bodily* ailments. They recover that is from an illness or from an operation more rapidly or more completely, and often recovering fully when that seems an unlikely outcome. It's important to add that the phrase that Dr. Benson used to describe this healing process, '*remembered wellness,*' carries its own implicit message. It so accurately describes the physical healing process as being mentally stimulated; not so much mind over matter perhaps, but mind aiding matter.

More recent research has gone considerably further. The more we learn about it, the more closely intertwined the mind-body interaction is seen to be. It has been demonstrated for example that even on a moment to moment basis, as we go about our daily lives, there is a direct link between our emotions, what we are feeling in our heads so to speak, and the *effective functioning* of the heart. Our own experience might well suggest this to us in any case, but what this research indicates is that during times of extreme mental stress and powerfully negative emotions such as heightened anger or grief, the actual effectiveness of the heart as a pumping machine is noticeably reduced. It simply cannot work at its best. Whereas when we are in the grip of positive emotions such as optimism or joy, or indeed when patients are encouraged to lift their spirits and try to concentrate on positive and constructive emotions, the heart too is seen to be in its most flexible and responsive state.

Happiness makes the heart beat longer

And if we take a longer term view, there are now many studies that suggest that a continued low or negative life state is associated with the possibility of quite widespread deterioration in bodily systems. Different researchers have highlighted different physiological effects, but the National Institute for Mental Health in the USA for example, includes in its various studies such conditions as a generally weakened immune response to illness and increased risk of such serious ailments as heart disease and strokes, cancer and diabetes. It's important to add that the *actual mechanisms* at work in these situations are still scarcely understood, but the *link* is now well established between what one might call a low life state, and many physical bodily ailments.

The great and good news is that the converse has also been shown to be true. As one medical scientist has expressed it, lifting your spirits can be potent medicine. And there is an increasing body of evidence to support the view that a strongly optimistic and positive approach to life not only boosts the body's immune system, and so strengthens our ability to resist or overcome illness, but again, on an everyday basis, it can lower blood pressure and can lead to a better regulated heart. Happiness if you like can make the heart beat longer!

But how should we view this growing body of scientific and medical research from a Buddhist point of view. It would seem at the very least that the discipline and regularity of a daily Buddhist practice places a very powerful tool in our hands, since it delivers to us the awareness that we can choose. Everyone of course has the power of choice, but it is the *awareness* of that fact that alone makes it meaningful, particularly in relation to our state of mind. That is the key issue.

Every day in our practice we can *choose* to transform the negativity in our lives, which we now know can have such potentially damaging long term effects on our physiological health. Every day we can make the cause to shift our life state towards the positive end of the spectrum, which we now know brings with it so many healthful benefits. And it's clear that a Buddhist practice can also open up a very much wider view of what it is that actually constitutes good health. So we become conscious of it not simply as the *absence* of sickness or anxiety at any particular point in time, but rather the *continued presence* of a strong and positive life state that underlies our sense of well being, that we can choose to boost and strengthen every single day.

—◆—

CHAPTER THIRTEEN

Changing the Wiring Diagram

Some years ago a scientist at the Harvard medical School[1] carried out what has since become regarded as something of a landmark experiment. He persuaded a group of volunteers who weren't musicians of any kind, to try to learn how to play a short, five-finger exercise on the piano. So each day for five days they came into his laboratory and sat down at the piano and went through the basic discipline of practising the exercise. They tried to keep to a strict metronome speed for example, and to play the music as accurately and as musically as possible. It may have seemed a somewhat bizarre situation, and no doubt it was to some extent, science often moves in such mysterious ways.

But for everyone who had volunteered for this weird bit of research, there was clearly a very considerable amount of concentration and application involved in simply struggling to get their fingers to move in a particular way, to perform a relatively complex routine which they had never been called upon to master before. Each day, after they had carried out the exercise the volunteers were given a form of brain scan to examine the effect on the area of the brain that controlled the finger movements. It happens to be called the motor cortex but that's not significant for this particular look at the experiment. What is highly significant however was that at the end of the five days the area of the brain allocated to controlling these fingers as they struggled to perform a new task, had increased. That is to say, the process of training these musically untrained fingers had *physically* changed the way that particular area of the brain was wired up. And the change had taken place in as short a period as five days.

That in itself was already a surprising result, since this experiment, along with several others that were carried out at around the same time, revealed a wholly new insight. Namely that the developed or adult brain seemed to be infinitely more flexible and malleable than had hitherto been believed. As we grow older and, as the stereotype would have it, much more set in our values and behaviour, the brain it seems, far from losing its flexibility as was thought to be the case, retains it to a remarkable degree. We retain that is the ability to re-shape the brain by the new choices that we make and the new skills that we learn.

The received wisdom that had held sway for many decades prior to this batch of studies was that by the time we reach early adulthood we are pretty much stuck with the brain that we have developed by that time. The general view was that the brain's form and functioning, the bits allocated to particular activities, and most important of all, the way they are connected up, or the wiring diagram as it might be called, were fixed in place, and would more or less remain that way for much of the rest of our lives.

The Harvard studies, along with several others, now suggested that we could re-train, and most importantly we could *go on re-training* the brain very much as we can train and modify muscles in the body. So it was a result that opened up a wholly new vision of how the adult brain functions. What's more, it opened up the possibility that we might retain this ability to re-mould and re-shape the brain, well on into our adult and advanced years.

The power of thought

As if that result were not surprising enough, the Harvard neuroscientist went on to modify even further our understanding of how the brain goes about its business. He arranged for a second group of volunteers to go through a similar research-training programme, but this time without the piano! That is to say he got them to do exactly the same five-finger exercise, but *in thought only*. He gave them the same musical briefing, the same exercise, and asked them to *think* their way through it on the same daily basis for five days. So these volunteers were asked to sit there, fingers still, hands still, but concentrating deeply on reading the music and imagining how they would move their hands and their fingers in order to play the piano and create the music.

The experiment was bizarre. The result was astounding. When this second research group were put through the same brain scanning process it was found that the same region of the brain had been modified in almost exactly the same way as the brains of those who had actually moved their fingers. That is to say, simply *thinking about* or imagining the movement of the fingers, had re-shaped or re-organised if you will, that area of the brain, in precisely the same way as actually going through the action of moving the fingers.

The results of this extraordinary experiment have since received confirmation in several different ways. There is for example a well known series of pictures from an MRI scan of the brain that show that exactly the same areas of the brain 'light up,' when we are merely *thinking* about a face or a place, as when we are actually using the complex physiological processes of our eyes to look at a photograph of a face or a place, or indeed the real thing. It adds a whole new dimension doesn't it, to our understanding of just how *real* our emotional response is when it is triggered by a fleeting memory of a loved one or a much loved place?

The power of choice

As you might expect these and similar research findings have profound implications for our understanding of how we function as thinking beings in all sorts of ways, both medical and social. It has implications for example, on the approaches to rehabilitation after someone has suffered a stroke or a brain injury. It is now widely recognised that it is possible to set high targets for recovery. Even complete recovery has been achieved in some cases, as the brain is trained to re-organise, or often re-organises itself, to form new pathways, new connections, around the areas of loss or damage.

But what about ordinary everyday life? What are the key implications you might ask of this remarkable new understanding, for the particular journey that we are on, seeking to understand the roots of human happiness? The new insight is still too new for neuroscientists, let alone the rest of us, to grasp all its implications, but it does seem, even to the extent that it is understood at present, that the basic situation is clear enough. Put simply it is that neuroscientists now have not the slightest doubt that if we have sufficient commitment and determination we can change profoundly the way the brain is wired up and therefore how it functions, through the new values and attitudes and new skills we *choose* to adopt or learn.

So we come back yet again, to the immense power of our personal choice.

What's more it seems that it's never too late to start. To use a close physical analogy, just as it's never too late to take a body to the gym, to give it a regular workout, and keep the muscles and the cardio-vascular system functioning more efficiently so, we now know, it's never too late to give the mind a spiritual work out.

We can learn hope and optimism
So at one extreme it would seem to open up wonderfully hopeful new approaches to treating life-diminishing disorders such as chronic depression. At the other it seems that qualities that are absolutely fundamental to a solid sense of stability and resilience and well being in our lives, qualities such as empathy and altruism and compassion and hope, are not in any way fixed in our make up, we only have what we happen to have developed so far you might say. The evidence is that they can be learned and increased and grown and developed until they play a much more active and contributing role in our lives, right the way through our adult lives. The choice is ours.

Hope and optimism as a way of life can become a matter of determination, rather than just a wish. And as Daniel Goleman expresses it in *Emotional Intelligence,* hope can be a potent ally in life;

'Hope, modern researchers are finding, does more than offer a bit of solace amid affliction; it plays a surprisingly potent role in life,

offering an advantage in realms as diverse as school achievement and bearing up in onerous jobs. Hope in a technical sense is far more than the sunny view that everything will turn out all right.'[2]

And what is undoubtedly extraordinary in this precise context, is just how often the lessons and the methods that have been evolved within Buddhism over so long a period, have been shown to play a powerful role in enabling people to move their lives in this radical way, from basically negative, down-casting, life-diminishing positions, to positive, uplifting and life-enhancing ones.

There are very clear studies to support this contention. From the fascinating and rapidly growing field of Cognitive Behavioural Therapy for example, where people with strong and deeply-rooted anxieties and phobias can be taught how to confront and challenge their fear and their negativity directly. Where is this negativity coming from? What is it based on? Why am I feeling it now? And by learning how to challenge it in this way they can learn how to manage it, or indeed overcome it, so that eventually they are able to go about their daily lives with greater confidence and stability and a greater sense of self worth. So there is a clear resonance here with what we seek to achieve with a daily Buddhist practice, in terms of learning how to challenge and *transform* negative emotions and impulses and responses, into positive ones. Indeed behavioural therapists have not infrequently adopted or adapted Buddhist methods, although of course, without any overtly religious dimension.[3]

We also have the fascinating research carried out by neuroscientists such as Richard Davidson at the University of Wisconsin, exploring this very specific thesis that fundamental life states such as optimism and compassion are mental skills that we can learn and enhance. We can that is *train* ourselves to be more positive and optimistic and hopeful, and indeed to have an enduring sense of happiness in our lives.

One treads carefully of course in drawing any major conclusions from these studies that associates them in any way with a specifically Buddhist approach to life, because that was no part of their purpose as research projects. But once again there would seem to be a clear echo, to go no further than that, of a long held Buddhist understanding that a happiness dimension, or the establishment of a positive, hope-filled sense of well being, is a skill that can be both *learned and improved with training.*

What about ordinary people like us?

But there is clearly a substantial question mark that hovers over the heart of that conclusion. Might it only apply to a very special, self-selected group of people, such as Buddhist monks, who have dedicated years of their life to mastering profound mindfulness skills? Or, if not going quite to that extreme, might it only apply to people who are prepared to go to very considerable lengths indeed to master so valuable a skill? We all know that to achieve a high level of proficiency in any field you care to think of, from a professional golf swing to performing on a classical guitar, can require a quasi-monastic level of commitment and dedication.

But what hope is there for the rest of us? What about ordinary people with only ordinary powers of commitment and dedication, not to mention a busy time-slicing life at work and with the family? How might ordinary people like us get on?

That in essence is the question that has lain behind much of the research life of the renowned psychologist at the University of Massachusetts, Jon Kabat-Zinn. He has spent much of the past 30 years or so, carrying out studies into the effect of what one might call mind training, on the way people function in ordinary daily life. So he has looked at the effects of such training for example on everything from people's immune systems to something as everyday as people's ability to handle stress in the working environment. Something we have all experienced at some stage in our lives.

In one particular study that is particularly relevant to the road we are travelling on, he involved a sizeable group of people holding down ordinary day jobs at various levels in a typical commercial organisation. So people absolutely like most of us. He first put all the people taking part through a series of well-proven tests, to get a measure of what might be called their general base level of happiness or contentedness with their lives. He then split them into two groups, A and B. Group A was basically put on hold as the control group, and given no special training. Group B was given a basic course in mindfulness training once a week for a period of just two months.

Very briefly, mindfulness training is based on a remarkable combination of modern cognitive science and classical Buddhist techniques. Basically it involves a series of mental exercises and is designed to enable people to develop a much more sensitive level of awareness of their life state. The whole idea is that they become more skilled at recognising and learning what they can do to move from a negative state, beset by negative emotions and responses, to a more positive life state. It has proved itself to be a very powerful method of mind training. As one psychologist has expressed it, it is possible to radically transform how we *experience* ordinary daily events by learning how to change the way we *pay attention* to them and therefore the *awareness* we generate in relation to them.

But back to the research study; for 8 weeks Group B was *learning* how to be more aware of how they behaved and responded in a range of situations, and they were asked to practice on their own on a daily basis. They were also asked specifically to focus on trying to be positive, and on practicing such qualities as patience with themselves, and compassion and gratitude. Meanwhile both groups went about their ordinary daily lives, commuting to work and shopping at the supermarket, cuddling their kids and watching the ball game on a Saturday afternoon, worrying about the credit card bill or the overdraft or whatever.

At the end of the eight weeks he put both groups, A and B, through the same battery of tests to assess what difference if any, had occurred to their general sense of well being and contentedness with their lives. The results can only be described as remarkable.

Group A remained where they had been all along at their original base level. The people in Group B however had experienced a very considerable change in their approach to life. They not only *felt* better and more positive and confident about their life state, but this feeling was confirmed by the fact that they scored markedly higher results on their responses to the so-called happiness tests. What's more, the effects of the training they had been through persisted several months after the project had been completed. They had so to speak *trained themselves* to be more positive, and in doing so had *become* substantially happier.

And just to round off the study, the researchers were able to demonstrate that there had been a beneficial spin-off effect on the participant's general health. When the whole group was given a flu jab, those who had been given the mind training programme, Group B, developed a far higher immunity to the flu bug than their counterparts, which is if you like, a classic illustration of the mind-body effect we were discussing earlier on, the widespread evidence that a positive and optimistic state of mind has a powerful beneficial effect on the body's overall immune system.[4]

It works both ways

If, as now seems clear, the brain can, through training, be re-wired positively, to enable us to create what you might call a more positive and optimistic outlook on life, a better or greater self as Buddhism often expresses it, what about the downside? Are there examples of the brain being re-wired or re-shaped *negatively,* as a result of sustained negative inputs? This is an issue that has recently moved centre stage, as more and more parents report that their children seem to lack the ability to concentrate for more than a few minutes at a time, or that they can't take the trouble to communicate properly, or that they seem to be utterly addicted to their screens. A frequent comment often overheard between mothers waiting at the school gates for their children is that all their children seem to want to do is to get back to their screens to play video games,or communicate with their peers on rapid-fire social networking channels such as Facebook or Bebo or Twitter. Teachers in both primary and secondary schools talk frequently of a sharp decline in attention spans, and the inability of pupils to communicate with one another at any length.

Professor Susan Greenfield, noted neuroscientist from Oxford University, has taken up this very issue and believes it is serious enough to issue what amounts to a warning. She has expressed the view that a regular, extended, daily diet of fast-paced computer games or television game shows or the like cannot be regarded as a *neutral* experience. It can only have, she argues, a powerful modifying and conditioning effect. In particular she has noted just such effects as parents are worried about, the shortening of attention spans and the inability to concentrate for more than a few minutes at a time.[5]

Indeed, she has gone out of her way to use a very striking word to describe the potential effect of a regular daily diet of this kind. She argues that it is likely to '*infantilise*' the developing brain, in the sense that it would tend to take it back to the state of younger children who naturally seek instant gratification with bright lights and rapidly changing images and so on, and who have of course very short attention spans. She notes the similarity with autistic children, who also find it very hard to communicate with other people on a face-to-face basis, but who are often perfectly comfortable communicating via a computer screen.

A recent study in the USA by the Kaiser Family Foundation found for example, that American Children between the ages of 8 and 18 are now linked in to their cell phones and computers and television and video game systems for an extraordinary average of 7.5 hours a day, or over 50 hours a week. Professor Greenfield has gone so far as to suggest that this profound change in the intellectual and visual diet of today's children could well have radical and lasting effects in terms of brain re-wiring.

'*It is hard to see,*' she has written, '*how living in this way on a daily basis will not result in brains, or rather minds, different from those of previous generations.*'[6]

A wake up call

As if to substantiate Professor Greenfield's argument, in March 2010 a specialist clinic in London launched the country's first dedicated programme of *therapy* to help children addicted to surfing the internet and playing computer games. The Capio Nightingale Hospital will offer residential care to children as young as 12, to enable them to overcome their overwhelming addiction to the computer screen. Parents talk of some children playing interactive games well into the small hours, who fly into an uncontrollable rage if they are told to switch off their screens. Other symptoms of this powerful addiction include sleep disorders and depression and fatigue, and a sense of isolation from what is going on around them.[7]

I suggest all that adds up to a sharp wake up call. But it's not just applicable to children is it? Other researchers in the field have noted just how much our adult lives are increasingly *dominated* by fast-paced communications technologies. Cell phones and blackberries and laptops and the internet fill our days with an endless bombardment of information and communication. Millions of people experience the constant nagging need to check for the very latest text message or e-mail. Millions more feel the compulsion to stay in constant touch with their sites on Facebook or My Space or Linked In.

We are you might say, constantly, compulsively *linked in,* and this compulsion prompts the obvious question, are we being served by these powerful technologies, or are we becoming increasingly enslaved by them, very much to the detriment of our own sense of well being?[8]

There is in fact a remarkable synthesis between the effects that Professor Greenfield warns us about, and the import of a passage from what is essentially a text book about interpreting or applying the Buddha's teaching to life in the modern world. This particular passage is about the effect of the stuff, or the 'toxins' as they're called here, that we take in every day from the 24/7 news and media communications machine.

'If after reading the newspaper, hearing the news, or being in conversation, we feel anxious or worn out, we know we have been in contact with toxins. Movies are food for our eyes, ears and minds. When we watch TV, the programme is our food. Children who spend five hours a day watching television are ingesting images that water the negative seeds of craving, fear, anger and violence in them. We are exposed to so many forms, colours, sounds, smells, tastes, objects of touch, and ideas that are toxic and rob our body and our consciousness of their well being. When you feel despair, fear or depression it may be because you have ingested too many toxins through your sense impressions. Not only children need to be protected from violent and unwholesome films, TV programmes, books, magazines and games. We too can be destroyed by these media.'[9]

The need for awareness

It's important to add I think, that in no way is this a call for anything resembling censorship, or any inhibition of what is called perhaps euphemistically, the freedom of the press. It is simply a call for greater *awareness* on the part of the reader, or the viewer, or the receiver of the inputs, of their potential effects on his sense of well being. We are bombarded by this stuff every day, as part of our constant contact with our environment. And we do clearly have a need to keep in touch with what is going on in our complex and frequently troubled local and global societies. All this passage is suggesting, I would argue, is that we also need to be mindful of the impact of this constant stream of images and words, often deliberately sensationalised images and words, on our brains and on our minds. It has been well demonstrated that constant exposure to brutality… brutalises. Similarly constant exposure to sensationalised news and gossip… de-sensitises.

The stream won't of course be turned off. If anything it can only increase, as more technologies are launched for firing information at us, whether we seek it or not, at any time of the day or night, anywhere we are in the world. It just helps I think to be aware, as both Professor Susan Greenfield and the Buddhist teacher express it, that all this stuff is not neutral, it's not *passive* in that sense. It is highly active, and it has a powerful effect on how we think and feel and view the world. And all this passage is saying is that the awareness places in our hands the weapon of choice, to protect ourselves against the negative effects and to strengthen the positive ones.

—ɷ—

CHAPTER FOURTEEN

A Kind of Revolution

Popular mythology has it that the new science of happiness was born only about a decade ago, as part of the outcome of an informal conference of some leading American psychologists, held in Mexico early in 1998. Like most mythologies it may have only a kernel of truth at its heart, but even if it is only a part of the story, it undoubtedly serves to underline the startling revolution that the field represents. For almost its entire history in the western world, ever since the time of Sigmund Freud, psychology has focused its attention on what ails and disables the human mind, from anxieties and depressions to chronic delusions. That has been its primary hunting ground, and its purpose might be described as seeking to bring its patients from a negative and disabled state, towards a more able and normal one. It has been argued in its defence that the medical community has a natural tendency to study pathology, or what is wrong with us, rather than what is right, and psychologists have simply followed in that well-trodden path.

Professor Martin Seligman, senior psychologist from the University of Pennsylvania, the inspiration behind that informal conference, and thus in a sense the father of the new school of positive psychology as it is now called, bluntly described that classical approach as seeking to bring patients, *'from a minus five to a zero.'* And he went on to use that same mathematical metaphor to characterise the crucial distinction between the classical and the radically new approach he was seeking to promote,

'It wasn't enough,' he said, *'for us to nullify disabling conditions and get to zero. We needed to ask, what are the enabling conditions that make human beings flourish? How do we get from zero to plus five.'*[1]

Even now, a dozen or so years on, it's hard to think of a more concise or more accurate metaphor to describe the radical new approach. Just as physical health should not defined as the mere absence of illness, so mental health, it argues, cannot be described as the mere *absence* of disabling anxieties. It is from just such a starting point that psychological studies can make a powerful contribution to people's lives by exploring the breadth and depth of *well being*, by understanding more fully the kinds of things that enable people to feel good about themselves, and their lives and their relationships.

However attractive that story is, it's important to stress that this wasn't by any means a wholly unexplored territory. There had been a relatively small number of explorers such as Edward Diener from Illinois and Daniel Kahneman from Princeton who had already made substantial tracks across bits of it, and uncovered many interesting things. And Buddhism of course has been talking to us for so long about the roots of human happiness. But the voice of Buddhism of course is not yet so loud or so listened to in the West.

Cascade of new knowledge

But what transpired after the Mexican meeting was almost unprecedented in any field. Suddenly, within the space of a few years there was an explosion of research studies by eminent psychologists and sociologists. If we add to these rich new insights coming out of positive psychology, the extraordinary cascade of new knowledge that is coming from the various fields of neuroscience and brain studies that we discussed earlier, it all adds up to the fact that we are in a sense a most favoured generation. So that we now have what even a handful of years ago would have seemed unthinkable, a burgeoning science of happiness, which delivers into our hands a wholly new perspective, a new set of markers to guide us as we try to understand what does, and equally important of course, *what does not*, make people feel satisfied with their lives.

That is undoubtedly, a kind of revolution. For the very first time in human history we have objective and physiological studies to illuminate what has always been the most subjective and slippery and elusive of fields. And, again for the first time, we can genuinely begin to define the implications of our happiness or it's absence…our feelings of sadness or depression…for other aspects of our life. When a person says that they feel happy or pleased or satisfied with life for example, that not only ties in with activity in the 'happiness' areas of the brain that we've been talking about, but we now know that it's linked to improved body chemistry and lower heart rate and blood pressure. When we make the effort to express gratitude to others it not only increases our overall sense of well being, it also lowers our stress hormones. Happiness we now know for sure, rather than just instinctively, is an *all body emotion.* It *is* very good for your health.

So what do the positive psychologists tell us?

The role of the positive psychologists is observational rather than prescriptive. That is to say they carry out studies to increase our understanding of the kinds of things that tend to make us feel good or better about ourselves and our lives, rather than laying down anything resembling a set of rules that we are supposed to follow to achieve well being. Those observations can then of course be embodied in various therapies. Several studies have shown for example that something as seemingly simple as getting people to keep a *gratitude journal,* has turned out to have real value in lifting people's spirits. Just taking the time once a week or so, to notice the things that we feel genuinely grateful for, can give a powerful boost to the sense of well being.[2] It is in that sense I think, that this work opens up a wholly new perspective. It enables us if we wish, to test out our view of life, or the approach to life that a Buddhist practice encourages us to follow, and see where we sit in relation to the kind of observations that have come out of the studies.

The wealth delusion

So what kinds of understanding are emerging? Well, one of the earliest, and most often repeated, and in some ways one of the most surprising findings, was that wealth, how much money we earn, isn't in any way a big, let alone a dominant factor in our basic sense of well being. Studies throughout the western-way-of-life parts of the world, taking in Europe and Japan for example as well as the USA, over many decades, have revealed this somewhat surprising fact. It seems that although we spend so much effort and energy in seeking to accumulate wealth, as if our very lives, let alone our happiness, depended upon it, the fact is that once our basic needs have been met, additional wealth seems to have very little to do with how fundamentally happy we are, or not. We deal with what might well be called this *wealth delusion* in detail, in the next chapter.

But when the positive psychologists move on to describe the kinds of values and behaviour that generate a profound sense of well being and stability and confidence in people, the sort of things that make people and societies work harmoniously, it is I think immediately apparent just how closely they echo and mirror the kinds of values and behaviour that lie at the very heart of Buddhist teachings. Let me just mention half a dozen key findings.

The uplifting power of compassion

They place right at the top of the tree for example, the powerful happiness effect within our own lives of compassion and altruism, of developing a fundamentally *giving* rather than a *taking* approach to life. It has been shown clearly that even quite small gestures bring immense benefits in terms of a personal sense of well being. From offering a smile or a word of encouragement or support on the spur of the moment for example, all the way up to investing the energy and the commitment to concern ourselves more deeply with the needs and anxieties and happiness of others, rather than concentrating, as we so readily tend to do, on our own current clutch of problems.

There is much discussion in the research findings of the remarkable transforming power of gratitude, unlocking, as it has been described, a whole *cascade* of beneficial effects both for the giver and the receiver. Going out of our way to express gratitude to someone has been shown to have a positive effect on our sense of well being sometimes for days after the event itself. Buddhism of course speaks of gratitude as being nothing less than the *starting point* of happiness.

They talk of the immense value of coming to know more clearly what our strengths are, and indeed our weaknesses, so that we are better placed to build our lives around the strengths, rather than being constantly anxious about the weaknesses. This immensely *practical* kind of self-knowledge or wisdom clearly can have a huge impact on our relationships in all the various roles we fill as partners and parents, as friends at play and colleagues at work, and it has a powerful underlying effect on our sense of self worth. Ruut Veenhoven for example, who happens to be one of the very few academics to actually occupy a chair of Happiness Studies at Erasmus University in Rotterdam, talks of the immense value of this kind of down-to-earth self awareness. He believes that one of the least talked about secrets of happiness is learning to like the life we have.

As an extension of that idea, these researchers talk of the importance of learning how to live in the *now,* making the very most of this moment, this conversation, this walk, this burst of sunshine on our face. Instead of, as we so often do, allowing ourselves to become wrapped up in anxieties about the past, or focused perhaps on some particular anticipated event in the future, postponing in a sense our present pleasure until some particular set of circumstances prevails. With our hugely active and restless minds this is not a skill it seems that comes to us easily, but once again, once we are aware of it, we can begin learn how to do it.

They talk of the hugely beneficial effect of having some meaningful goal or direction that is bigger and wider than the simple daily progression of our lives, something that we have to strive for, so that it stretches us and lifts us up out of our daily routine. Martin Seligman describes this approach as *'the meaningful life,'* and in his view it can deliver a very high levels of satisfaction with our lives. Buddhism I might add, is constantly encouraging us to set genuine goals for ourselves to develop a bigger and broader life and to focus on creating value both in our own lives and the lives of those whom our life touches.

And perhaps above all they talk of the importance of a sense of connectedness or engagement as they call it, a real sense of involvement in the lives of family and friends and work colleagues as a constant reminder of our wider humanity. This turns out to be in many ways *the* fundamental ingredient in a well balanced and happy life. The evolutionary biologists tell us that we are in our deepest nature a gregarious animal, that we survive and flourish because of our ability to live and work and co-operate in family and tribal groups. The positive psychologists tell us that we flourish as we learn how to develop lasting and fulfilling and harmonious relationships with the wider circle of those whom our lives touch. When we manage to create or experience these harmonious relationships they don't simply make us feel good about ourselves, they buttress and reinforce all our creative energies and we become empowered so to speak, to pursue many other fulfilling objectives in our life.

Just common sense
Whenever I set out that all too brief exposition of what has been derived from a vast amount of social research over the past dozen or so years, as a theme for group discussion for example, the response is often that it's all just common sense. If you have all those things in your life, the comment tends to go, then your bound to be happy, of course you are.

I can only agree. Indeed it is very often argued by Buddhists that Buddhist values and principles are essentially common sense. Buddhism is reason they say.

But that response doesn't really go far enough. It's important to be absolutely clear what we have here. We have modern social science research, defining the qualities that make people feel good about their lives, the qualities that help people and societies to work harmoniously, in terms that any practising Buddhist would immediately recognise, since they echo many of the principles and values that lie at the very centre of a Buddhist approach to life.

But what about our genes?

It's an important question isn't it, how much of our capacity for happiness is in a sense beyond our control, either way, good or bad, since it has been inherited from our forebears? Dylan Evans, sociologist at the University of Bristol, in his book *Emotion: The Science of Sentiment*, puts forward the fascinating proposition that the *default* position in human nature, if I may put it that way, must be towards optimism and happiness, rather than towards sadness and depression.[3]

The basic thrust of his argument is that evolution will undoubtedly have favoured the selection of any qualities that enabled our ancestors to establish close and supportive relationships. Key relationships that is, with mating partners and offspring and others in the tribal group, because they are precisely the qualities that would have made a huge difference in helping them to survive in harsh and difficult conditions, and of course to reproduce. Those qualities, he suggests, by definition would have been positive rather than negative. So he argues, that's precisely why our ability to establish those kinds of positive relationships today, is so deeply tied up with our personal sense of satisfaction and well being. It is an illuminating idea that seems to make a great deal of sense, and in several ways it does tie in with other bits of research.

The happiness set point

Several years ago for example David Lykken, from the University of Minnesota, added a new dimension to happiness research. He put forward the startling idea that we all have pretty much a happiness *set point* in our lives. It can be high or low, this set point, it varies widely he suggests from individual to individual. There is no precise analogy, but we might think about it perhaps as being similar to the way in which we all have a personal metabolic rate, a rate at which we burn up energy, which has a very substantial impact on our body mass index. Some people we know can eat like the proverbial horse and stay as thin as a bean pole. Others talk of putting on weight even if they eat four lettuce leaves. Similarly, we can all readily identify in our environment those people who have a sunny, easygoing nature, and an innate ability to smile their way through any amount of stress and anxieties. While others are the reverse, seeming to have an in-built knack of being aware of the downside in just about every situation. And of course there is every conceivable graduation in between.

Lykken's radical analysis came after an extensive study, as a result of which he came to two important propositions, propositions rather than conclusions notice. One was that a very *substantial* proportion of our innate sense of well being, our basic satisfaction or dissatisfaction with our lives is likely to be inherited, we get it handed down to us in our genes. The second was that we probably have a basic level of happiness, or a *happiness set point* as he called it, which is more or less fixed. We have to make do with what we are given. We can't substantially increase our happiness index, any more if you like, than we can radically change our metabolic rate.

Lykken's propositions were provocative enough to stimulate a huge amount of research over the following years. Without getting submerged in too much detail, studies in the USA and Europe for example, have involved people who have been through really challenging, life-threatening situations such as losing a limb in an accident, or fighting off cancer. In both situations the sufferers returned to their happiness norm so to speak, in a remarkably short time, a matter of weeks rather than months. These people were even able to speak of living more intensely and with a greater awareness of their blessings as a result of their ordeal. Psychologist Edward Diener from Illinois, has identified two situations, namely the loss of a spouse and the loss of a job, where the period of suffering is very much longer, extending over several years. But nevertheless, even in these circumstances he eventually found that there is a return to a sort of happiness norm.

I must say that simply reading these studies of how people have overcome such great challenges in their lives and returned to a profound stability, even happiness, generates immense respect for the sheer power of the human spirit.

At the other extreme, the upside so to speak, researchers haven't been able to come up with anything like the same quality of human experience. We are left with the comparative banality of the *lottery moment* as it's been called. All the studies seem to show that despite the steep spike of elation at the moment of winning, it doesn't last. Lottery winners too, return to their set point.

So after several years and multiple research studies, what sort of conclusions have been reached? The research over the intervening years by members of the positive psychology network, and indeed by David Lykken himself, suggests two absolutely crucial corrections. One, that the proportion of our *optimism,* if I may use that as the sort of portmanteau happiness word, that is hardwired into our make up through inheritance, is very much less than was believed, perhaps as little as 25%. The second, that nothing is fixed in place, that our inheritance and the happiness set point can be changed, built upon, improved, by the *attitudes* and the *approach to life* that we learn to adopt.

That is an immensely positive finding isn't it? It seems that wherever we look in this wide range of studies we find powerful support for this view that we can indeed train and teach ourselves in various ways, to improve profoundly and radically our capacity in life for optimism, and well being and satisfaction with our lives.

It brings us back directly to the understanding that lies at the very heart of Mahayana Buddhist teachings, namely that the level of happiness in our lives is essentially a matter of choice. It's up to each one of us. It's not a matter of chance or accident or luck, as we so often take for granted. It's a matter of choice. And Buddhism certainly teaches that we can all without exception, take hold of our lives and learn how to make that choice.

The tough question

But of course, *knowing* about that idea isn't the same as *living it*. Knowing about those happiness factors that we've been discussing, isn't the same as *having* them in our lives is it? Similarly, knowing about the possibility of choice, isn't in any way the same as *having* the courage and the wisdom to make that choice. Indeed one of the elements that I personally miss most from many of these studies is the idea of the *struggle* that is involved. Because in my experience it is a struggle to live in this way, it takes real energy and perseverance to consistently challenge the negative and look for the positive in all the situations we encounter, good bad and indifferent. Just as it takes real courage and commitment to determine to create value out of all the situations we encounter, the indifferent and the bad, as well as the good.

So you might ask, how do we move forward? How do we progress from understanding the value of the basic idea, to building this optimism that both Buddhist texts and the positive psychologists talk about so much, as an active and daily dimension in our lives?

The Buddhist answer to that tough question is that we can't simply *think* our way into a new frame of mind, or a new approach to life. We can't achieve it if you like by sheer force of will or intellect, however forcefully we have been educated to believe that we can. We have to take the right action. And if we squeeze it down into a nutshell, that in essence, is what *all* Buddhist practice is about. It is the action tailored to the need. It is that personal, daily, life time training programme that has been fashioned and put to the test over many centuries, in the toughest testing ground of them all…real life.

In essence, as I mentioned earlier, it's not all that different from a personal fitness programme at the gym, to improve our physical fitness. Only here we are talking about spiritual muscle and about developing an emotional resilience. It's purpose is to show us how to take the unlikely and challenging material out of which all our lives are fashioned, and transform it into the stuff of hope and optimism and confidence and well being. Although the grass always seems greener in everybody's else's garden, every human life, however brilliant and scintillating and pain free it might seem from the outside, involves fear as well as hope, despair as well as joy on the inside. So at the heart of the Buddhist vision is this promise that it is indeed possible to strengthen our ability to see all the things in our lives... that's right, all the things...the fear as well as the hope, the despair as well as the joy, from a positive, constructive, optimistic point of view.

The reality of the vision

And the promise is real. Indeed what I find utterly fascinating is just how much that sort of realistic, down-to-earth language is being echoed in some of the very latest papers coming out of positive psychology. Professor Martin Seligman for example, who I've mentioned earlier, has talked of how a sense of optimism has to be broad and deep enough to *embrace* the sad and the painful. He also talks of consciously setting out to pour our energies into the positive, learning more about our strengths, and building on them to buttress the sense of well being in our lives, rather than using up our energies on simply trying to improve our weaknesses.

In his latest book, *The Pursuit of Perfect*, Professor Tal Ben-Shahar,[4] who for many years taught one of the most popular courses at Harvard, the positive psychology course, has come to very similar conclusions. He talks for example of the need to *get real.* Being optimistic he argues, isn't about being eternally cheerful. Not at all. That would be hugely unreal. It is about learning how to build a sense of hope and optimism by getting to grips with, getting up close to, embracing the pains and problems we encounter, so that we genuinely understand them. He talks also of the immense value that we can generate in our lives from learning how to look for the *seeds* of the positive even in the things that go badly wrong in our lives, rather than continually being eaten up by the negative effects.

The transforming power of optimism

Those sorts of phrases I suggest could very easily appear in a Buddhist commentary, given that optimism is such an important part of the Buddhist approach to life. Indeed, one of the things that struck me most when I first took up a Buddhist practice was the powerful sense of optimism there was at discussion meetings and seminars, even when people were talking about all kinds of everyday difficulties and problems. Life for these people it was clear, was very much about *getting real,* about seeing the problems for what they were, and challenging them, rather than being cast down by them. Ordinary people that is, with ordinary everyday problems, learning to see life differently through the focusing lens of a Buddhist practice.

And the greatness of a Buddhist practice in my view, is precisely that, its immense practicality. It delivers into our hands a method that enables us to achieve just a slight shift in perspective from negative to positive, and strange as it may seem, that is all that is needed. It may only be a slight change, but time and time again it proves to be enough to help us tackle the problem, or cope with the anxiety with a completely different attitude, that then leads on to tangible, positive outcomes.

It seems clear that there is nothing coming out of the new science of happiness that in any way conflicts with that view.

—◊—

The Wealth Delusion

We are very close to the end of this long journey towards a fuller understanding of what we mean by happiness. But we obviously can't close without at least a sidelong glance in the direction of what has been described by a leading English sociologist as the paradox that lies at the very heart of the western way of life. Namely the immense importance we attach to the role of money in any picture of happiness we paint for ourselves. The longing for the kind of happiness that it's believed only money can bring, is deeply embedded in the western psyche.

A recent article in a popular but genuinely scientific journal, carried the sub-heading, *Why money messes with your mind.*[1] The title alone carries a very significant message. Economists may go on regarding money dispassionately, as very much an impersonal medium of exchange, invented in its various forms throughout history simply to make the whole business of trade and markets and buying and selling flow more smoothly. But almost nobody else does. In ways that we probably don't think about too deeply, we recognise that money is much more than that, much darker, much more personal, closely linked in fact to all sorts of crucially important things such as our personal sense of self worth and our awareness of the status and power that money can bestow.

Indeed this particular article suggests that money, the pursuit of wealth in all it's aspects, can have very much the same sort of disorientating effect on people as a drug, leading to a similar kind of addiction. It goes on;

'Some studies, even suggest that the desire for money somehow gets cross-wired with our appetite for food. And of course, because having a pile of money means that you can buy more things, it is virtually synonymous with status...so much so that losing *it can lead to depression and even suicide.'[2]*

Messing with the mind indeed.

The noted English philosopher A.C. Grayling chose to entitle an essay on a similar theme, *'The Greed that will destroy us.'* And when you think about it that is not far off the historical Biblical passage which is usually given as *'money is the root of all evil.'* Although the actual passage carries a far more potent message, *'the love of money is the root of all evil.'[3]*

Not a marginal debate

So clearly there is a debate of sorts under way here, and undoubtedly it's not a marginal one. Whether or not we are prepared to acknowledge it, it would be strange wouldn't it, if we had not all been shaped and conditioned in some measure by this long-running, hard-driving, materialist consumerist environment that we all inhabit? Certainly it is one of the issues that those of us who happen to live in the western-way-of-life parts of the world can't really duck out of. Nor should we want to, given that the impact that money has on our general sense of satisfaction and contentedness with life is undoubtedly a big deal.

Put simply, the crux of the argument put forward by sociologists would seem to be that in western society today, we have largely replaced the pursuit of *meaning* in our lives for the mere pursuit of money. Exchanged genuine *quality* of life for mere standard of living. We have that is, wittingly or not, allowed the endless cycle of earning and spending, buying and acquiring, to become pretty much what our lives are about, our principal objective. The distinctive signature of our time.

Is that really what we want?

The Buddhist view
But let's start by looking at what might be called the Buddhist view. Since Buddhism claims to be about daily life, and since money is an integral part of the complexity of all our daily lives, Buddhism has somehow to cope with this particular bit of that complexity. In fact it has a great deal to say that is refreshingly direct about wealth, and how we might best relate to it. Perhaps the central point we need to hang onto, mainly because it runs counter in so many ways to the widely held stereotype, is that Nichiren Buddhism is not in any way about *giving things up*. It's not about diminishing or reducing or setting arbitrary limits on what we might or might not possess. Not at all. It teaches simply that since we clearly have extensive physical and spiritual needs, we have to attend to both if we are to achieve the most fulfilling and creative lives of which we are capable.

The physical needs are often described as earthly desires, with not the slightest sense of the derogatory attaching to that phrase.

They are essentially needs and wants that relate to the material dimension of our life, and they are clearly part and parcel of our sense of well being. Wanting things is part of our basic humanity, and has been ever since there have been things to want, from sharp stone hand axes and pretty cowry shells, to a better home and a better paid or more satisfying job, and on to a car that can carry the whole family, and more comfortable material circumstances.

So Buddhism teaches, we shouldn't in any way try to *reject* these wholly natural wants in our life, or see them as separate from, or somehow in conflict with, our basic spirituality. Indeed the reverse is true, they can become the strongest route to achieving our personal human revolution. In the sense that it doesn't really matter what it is that launches us down the road of establishing goals for our life, both material and spiritual, and then committing ourselves to the practice as a way of achieving them. The understanding that lies at the very heart of Buddhism is that this process will inevitably begin to draw out the perception that what we are really seeking in life is meaning, and a sense of confidence and a durable sense of well being, and the profound sense of self worth that comes from the exercise of compassion and altruism.

So where do we draw the line?

So where then do we draw the line between what makes sense for our lives, and what doesn't? The key thing is working hard to maintain a sense of *balance* between the spiritual and the material. Not getting swept away as if by a tidal wave, in one direction or the other. The trouble arises Buddhism argues, for us and for those around us, when the hunger for more stuff, more material goods, becomes a dominant or overwhelming life condition. We may not see it in that way, or we may not see it *early* enough, since these things tend to creep up on us. We may regard it as simply a powerful desire to get on in life. But when the drive for yet more possessions, yet more material wealth, becomes the overriding motivational force in our lives and we find ourselves driven to pursue it, with little or no concern for the effect on us, our values, and the lives of those around us, then, Buddhism teaches, we are way out of balance. And the effects can be far reaching. In fact Buddhism uses language not dissimilar to that in the scientific article that we touched upon a moment ago. It describes *greed,* because, let's face it, that's really what we are talking about here, as a *poison* or addiction in our system that can infect all the dimensions of our life and be the source of long lasting pain and suffering.

As a case in point, as I'm writing this the newspapers happen to be full of the truly tragic story of a 50 year old businessman. He was it seems a loving husband and father who became so mentally disabled by the suffering that came from impending bankruptcy, and the fear of losing all his manifold wealth and possessions that he had built up, that he became capable of actually shooting his wife and daughter, and then dying himself in the fire that he lit to destroy their family home. His possessions had become more important to him than life itself.

The startling paradox

That is of course an extreme example of the messing with the mind that money can bring about, but it does nonetheless bring us directly to the sort of work carried out over recent years by the sociologists, and the remarkable paradox that they have revealed. Most of us in the western-way-of-life parts of the world for example, are conditioned to believe that much of our happiness lies in seeking greater financial wealth. But the studies carried out by the social scientists over the past 50 to 60 years, in those same western-way-of-life parts of the world, reveal a startlingly different picture.

In fact one of the earliest, and most often repeated, and in some ways one of the most surprising findings of all this research has been that wealth, how much money you earn, *isn't* a substantial factor at all in our basic sense of well being. Once our basic needs have been met, additional wealth it seems has a rapidly diminishing role to play in how fundamentally happy we feel, until eventually it dies out altogether as a contributing factor. You could argue in fact that the modern research has gone a very long way indeed to proving the truth locked up in the well-worn adage that *you can't actually buy happiness.*

So surprising is this conclusion, that it has been described by one European sociologist as '*the paradox at the heart of modern western society.*'[4] Why a paradox? Because it seems to be so completely out of step with our current aggressively materialist, consumerist western culture, driven by the constant itch to acquire more stuff. We all know that we want to be rich or richer don't we? Because we all believe firmly that although it may not solve *all* the issues that trouble us, it will certainly blow most of them away. So we'll be happier…won't we?

The short answer comes out as a resounding no. What study after study has revealed is the sheer scale of that delusion. It's particularly ironic, not to say deeply troubling for all of us, that as I write these words the entire world is being compelled to live through an economic and financial cataclysm, created to a very large extent by the lust on the part of the very wealthy for even greater wealth. One example I read about recently involved the immensely wealthy, but now disgraced, American financier Marc Drier, currently serving a 20 year sentence for fraud. When he was asked by the judge at his trial why he had risked everything in hatching up yet another fraudulent scheme to make himself another $380 million dollars or so, he is quoted as responding, *'I thought it would make me happy.'*[5] Which suggests that all his existing multiple millions hadn't yet achieved that objective.

The paradox revealed

But very briefly, the social research seems clear. It shows that although populations in most western and westernised parts of the world have grown very much richer over the past fifty to sixty years, they haven't it seems, grown any happier. The wealth curve in those parts of the world rises steeply. The happiness curve rises scarcely at all. Indeed in some respects it declines because of something that has been defined as *reference anxiety.* Which is a somewhat inflated way of describing the anxiety stoked up by the efforts to keep up with the Joneses, as they demonstrate their greater wealth in various ways, buying bigger and flashier cars or more flat screen TV's and so on.

As the eminent economist from the London School of Economics, Professor Richard Layard has expressed it;

'There is a paradox at the heart of our lives. Most people want more income and strive for it. Yet as Western societies have got richer, their people have become no happier.

This is no old wives' tale. It is a fact proven by many pieces of scientific research. As I'll show, we have good ways to measure how happy people are, and all the evidence says that on average people are no happier today than people were fifty years ago. Yet at the same time average incomes have more than doubled. This paradox is equally true for the United States, and Britain and Japan.'[6]

So powerful is the paradox that most of us find it hard to accept, since most of us are in some measure caught up in it! We are so conditioned by the values of the societies that we have grown up in and competed in for so long. But we are undoubtedly flying in the face of an overwhelming body of evidence. Time and time again the researchers advise us to reject our conditioning and face up to the reality. As another sociologist Gregg Eastebrook makes clear;

'Over the past two decades, in fact, an increasing body of social science and psychological research has shown that there is no significant relationship between how much money a person earns and whether he or she feels good about life.'[7]

The materialist dead end

But in fact of course it's not limited to wealth is it? On almost any criterion we care to look at, in these western-way-of-life parts of the world we have more these days than ever before. More of just about everything; more comfort, more food, more houses, more health, more leisure, more partners. But not it seems more happiness.

So what kind of answers have the researchers come up with to explain this restless modern malaise? It's a complex question and there are of course several answers, but many of them have been lumped together under the heading of the *materialist dead end*. Psychologist Edward Diener, from the University of Illinois, and one of the prime movers in the field of positive psychology, has described this phenomenon as the *downside* of today's vastly greater affluence.[8] Professor Layard talks of it as *'the hedonic treadmill.'[9]*

It reveals its effects in many ways of course, but let me just mention two that seem to stand out above the rest. One is that there is so much more to be *hungered after* in our modern society, so much more on display in showrooms and shopping malls and supermarkets and so on, that it has become a powerful *external* cause of *inner* discontent. People actually experience a real sense of loss and deprivation and frustration, because they can't possess, can't carry away, more of this stuff that is on display. And I think that most of us can empathise with that situation. We've all been there to some extent.

The second is the fact that we are all constantly being called upon to measure ourselves these days, *who* we are and *what* we have, against an endless procession of supposed role models on film and television and in lifestyle magazines, who are presented as being highly successful and vastly better off, and therefore *by implication* happier. The equation seems to go unquestioned, success equals wealth equals happiness, although of course we all know that there is no such simple conjunction.

The psychologists tell us that comparison with others is a constant and immensely influential dimension in our lives, having a very real effect on our overall sense of self worth and our satisfaction or dissatisfaction with our own lives. And that of course is precisely the way the powerful modern marketing and advertising machine works, playing with great skill on our natural tendency to compare ourselves with these supposed role models, and so focus on what we *haven't got*, as opposed to what we have. In that sense the ever-present influence of modern lifestyle marketing is yet another powerful external cause of inner discontent.

So that in essence is the paradox revealed. It seems that it is the vastly greater *awareness* of other people's wealth and possessions which is so visible in today's western-style societies, that triggers not a measure of having made it, or a sense of satisfaction because of our own greatly improved circumstances, but the very reverse. The studies show it is now the source of a much wider sense of *dissatisfaction.* The whole process becomes in a sense a sort of self-defeating spiral as *reference anxiety* takes over, this constant tendency to compare ourselves with those who have more rather than with those who have less, chews away at our appreciation of all that we *do have.*

The itch to acquire

Buddhism talks to us a great deal about the very real threat that this constant tendency to compare ourselves with others can represent to our well being, steadily eating away at our sense of stability and self worth. Nichiren Daishonin for example, mentions it on numerous occasions in his letters.

' It is like the case of the poor man,' he writes,' who spends night and day counting his neighbour's wealth but gains not even half a coin.'[10]

But the remarkable thing for me, I have to say, is just how closely this very *modern* scientific analysis, of the unsettling effects of the constant itch to acquire more stuff, chimes with the *classic* Buddhist description of the life state of Hunger, which it describes as the cause of a great deal of self-inflicted pain and suffering. With the emphasis clearly on the fact that it is *self inflicted*, and can therefore be remedied. Hunger very briefly, is the life state in which we are convinced that our happiness lies in acquiring something which is, for whatever reason, just out of our reach. The agony lies in the fact that for people in this life state, there is *always* something… that is just out of reach. It embraces of course the vast range of material things on offer in the showroom windows, but it's not by any means limited to material things. It reaches out in every direction to the desire for status, and fame, and wealth, and partners, and on to permanent youth and beauty through plastic surgery. A modern social network such as Facebook for example even stimulates the desire to acquire and display more friends!

Not just envy

But the key point I want to make is that in no way should this be confused with simply envy of someone else's success. Its effect is far deeper and wider than that. If we can't achieve these acknowledged symbols of success we tell ourselves, what's wrong with us? Clearly we must be some sort of failure. We just don't have what it takes to succeed in life. And since in this equation, material success is the *only* route to happiness, we just don't have what it takes to be truly happy. Who we *are* if you like, has become synonymous with *what we have.*

And that's the crucial issue isn't it? For as long as our lives are taken up with stuff, we are essentially treating ourselves as material animals. But we are undoubtedly spiritual animals, however much we may try to persuade ourselves to the contrary. The physical and the material simply aren't enough, and for as long as we try to live as if they were, we know that we are in some measure *diminishing* ourselves, or in Buddhist terms, we are slandering ourselves.

A meaningful spiritual life

Once again Nichiren Daishonin nails this issue precisely when he writes in one of his letters, *more valuable than the treasures in any storehouse,* that is to say…stuff, *are treasures of the body*…that is to say good health, *and the treasures of the heart are most valuable of all*… that is to say, a meaningful spiritual life.[11]

And in our deepest selves we know that to be true don't we? Whenever we manage to pause from the pace and bustle and constant complexity of modern life and take stock, we know that we earnestly seek treasures of the heart in our lives, a deep sense of the *meaning and worth* of our lives, and meaningful relationships with all those whose lives touch ours.

And I think it's certainly possible to argue that that seeking is at least part of the reason why over the past 40 to 50 years, perhaps a shade longer, what might be called a quiet revolution has taken place. In that time frame many tens of thousands of people in Europe and the Americas and elsewhere, ordinary people like us, holding down a day job, falling in love and bringing up families, worrying how to pay the bills and caring for ageing relatives and so on, have chosen to put that all together under the umbrella of a Buddhist set of principles and values. It is so striking a development that it has been described by religious historians as a *new departure* in the history of religion.

Why? Because for the very first time in its history Buddhism is moving westwards, out of Japan and Asia, into Europe and the Americas and elsewhere, and it is moving not on the backs of missionaries, but pretty much by word of mouth, people speaking to people. So it is as I've said, a genuinely quiet revolution. But historically speaking it is immensely significant. Never before has Buddhism spread so rapidly or so widely geographically. Never before in the religious history of the West have so many people turned to Buddhism for answers to their queries on life the Universe and everything. The choice that Buddhism offers provides it seems, a meaningful resolution to the many challenges that modern life in the West presents. Meaningful, and happier indeed, since people in such large numbers clearly aren't turning to Buddhism because it makes them less happy!

It is possible to argue I think, that this quiet revolution, is one among several influences that is having a profound effect on the way we are learning to re-evaluate the idea of *success* in modern society, away from wealth towards more meaningful measures.

—∞—

CHAPTER SIXTEEN

A Brave New World

In 2008, President Sarkozy of France chose to throw a cat among the economic pigeons. He suggested that in the process of measuring their economic well being and development, as all nations try to do every year, all countries should attempt to factor in an evaluation of the national level of *happiness*. It was a startling moment, and few commentators were surprised, including perhaps Mr Sarkozy himself, when it was received with some amazement and a fair measure of cynicism around the world. But unabashed, he took the idea further and asked a number of leading economists in America and France to examine the idea further, including the Nobel Prize winning economist Amartya Sen of Harvard.

That is I suggest, an extraordinarily bold thing to have done. Indeed I don't think it's going too far to say that we could well be witnessing a key moment in our economic and social history, a moment that we might well look back on with immense pleasure, as marking a new beginning in how we evaluate what we mean by *success* in modern society. There is in fact one nation that already does try to establish a measure of national happiness every year, it is the tiny

Buddhist kingdom of Bhutan in the Himalayas. No one would suggest that Bhutan might in some way be a role model for the large and powerful industrialized nations of the world, or indeed for the many poorer and often struggling, developing nations. But just examine for a moment the alternative that those nations, indeed all nations universally, have adopted up till now as the prime indicator of their welfare and well being.

That alternative is known as Gross Domestic Product or GDP. It's an acronym that we have all heard a thousand times in political and economic discussions, so that we all tend to take it completely for granted as being…well… a very important something. We may not be quite sure what that something is, but we do know that it's important. We would certainly be correct in holding that view. In fact it has been described by economists as being, by a long way, the world's most powerful number, the most powerful *single numerical indicator.* Why? Because it has for many decades dominated the thinking certainly of Western governments, if not of all governments throughout the world, in taking fundamental decisions that affect all our lives.

It was invented by economists about 75 years ago, after the Great Global Depression of the 1930's, to provide some meaningful measure of general economic activity. But its influence has steadily grown over the years until it has become a kind of all-embracing indicator, a kind of instant shorthand way of defining a nation's *health and well being.* In fact it provides nothing of the sort. GDP is solely a measure of what is produced and what is bought and sold in trade. So that anything that involves money changing hands gets included, whatever the money changed hands for. Producing things in factories and delivering services like water and electricity of course. But its crucial failing is that it takes absolutely no account of the *effect* of producing those goods, or of *quality of life* or of *human interactions*. It fails to reflect the fact for example that some activity that may well contribute to GDP, does much harm rather than good to the world we all inhabit. It measures for example the value of goods but in no way does it take account of the environmental impact of their production in terms of pollution, or depletion of resources or the destruction of vast eco-systems such as the Amazon or the Indonesian rain forests.

Many leading thinkers have been aware of this huge anomaly at the heart of our society, and have brought it to our attention in various ways. As one Robert Kennedy for example, reminded all of us some 40 years ago, in the midst of some very troubled times,

'GDP counts napalm and the cost of a nuclear warhead and armoured cars for police who fight riots in our streets. It does not include the beauty of our poetry or the strength of our marriages; the intelligence of our public debate or the integrity of our public officials.' [1]

Or, he might have added, how we feel about our lives and our relationships, or the sense of living a full and meaningful and balanced life. But by and large those were lone voices. Today however there is a growing clamour from many directions. As one leading American economist, John Hall wrote recently,

'An over-reliance on GDP is not just misleading, it's harmful. Focusing on economic growth blinds policy makers to other measures of progress.' [2]

And here in the UK we have Professor Richard Layard, of the London School of Economics, posing the crucial question of what we should *change*, what we should do differently if, as a society, we were to decide that the time has now come to establish as one of our major goals, the achievement of a happier way of life. And when you think about it, what greater goal can there be for any society?

His primary answer is absolutely unequivocal;

'We should monitor the development of happiness in our countries as closely as we monitor the development of income.'[3]

The reason for this brief excursion into the tangled realm of political economics is to suggest that we happen to be living in very privileged times. We are witnessing if you like the slow building of a wave that could bring immense social change. What seems clear is that the fundamental question we posed at the beginning, namely what do we really mean when we talk about happiness, is no longer a marginal question, it is steadily moving to *centre stage*. Not just in our individual lives, where it has perhaps always been uppermost or thereabouts as a motivation, but as a matter of wider social debate.

Over the past ten or fifteen years for example, the discussion of what we meant when we talked about a sense of well being in our lives, what kinds of values and behaviour made people feel good about their lives and their relationships, has passed out of the hands of philosophers and religious teachers, into mainstream psychological and sociological studies. All the indications are that the circle of this debate is now widening to encompass *mainstream* political and economic thinking. The idea that there's much more to life than GDP, is no longer just a political quip. It defines the possibility of a radical change of direction in the kinds of choices we make, *as a society.* That is I believe, a crucial point, and it taps directly into an understanding that has always been at the heart of a Buddhist approach to life, the idea that the pursuit of a sense of well being at the individual level, has an infinitely wider and deeper social significance.

As Daisaku Ikeda, one of today's most perceptive thinkers and writers on Buddhism has expressed it,

'In an age when both society and the religious world are wrought by turmoil and confusion…' as indeed they are today…'*only a teaching that gives each individual the power to draw forth his or her Buddha nature can lead all people to happiness, and transform the tenor of the times. In other words… there can be no lasting solution to the problems facing society that does not involve our individual state of life.'*[4]

What we have been discussing in this book has focused, for the most part, on the way in which a Buddhist practice can help us as *individuals* to understand our lives and to develop happy and productive relationships, within a relatively close environment. The fact is of course that those are the relationships that have by far the biggest influence on our lives. They make up the fabric of our lives from day to day and from week to week. As we all know, maintaining harmonious relationships even within this relatively narrow compass takes considerable energy and effort.

But that having been said perhaps the biggest challenge now facing us as individuals is learning how to extend this understanding, this compassion that the practice helps us to develop, out beyond the circle of our friends and colleagues, out into a wider society, indeed out to a global society. At first hearing that may sound like no more than wishful thinking, but Buddhism teaches that the two are indivisibly intertwined, the individual and the social.

It argues that a fundamental change towards the *positive,* in a person's approach to life, has this enduring ripple effect, spreading out slowly, gradually through family and friends, into the local society and beyond. It is a powerful vision. Indeed Buddhism teaches that a movement towards a better society, based on the principles of respect for the lives and values of others, and with peace and individual happiness as its objectives, *cannot be created* as a top down process. It has to start from the bottom up, with a profound change taking place within the lives of countless individuals, gradually changing the way the whole of society functions.

And the change starts, Buddhism argues, with an altogether clearer understanding of the kinds of values and behaviour that enable individual people to feel good about themselves and their lives and their relationships. These are the very same values that make individuals and societies work more harmoniously. And they are the very same values that, as so many commentators have noted, are needed to meet this generation's unique challenge, learning how to live peacefully and sustainably in an extraordinarily crowded world.

That idea brings to us an infinitely broader and wider vision of what we really mean when we are talking about personal happiness. *No man is an island*. None of us is alone. Buddhism teaches that whatever our mind-set may be when we set out on this journey, merely seeking our own happiness can never be enough. We can never isolate ourselves from what is going on in other people's lives, no matter how strongly we may believe, or try to convince ourselves that we can. Thus the message at the heart of Buddhism is that lasting and durable and meaningful happiness of the kind that we are all seeking can only come from working to the very best of our abilities, to create those same qualities in the lives of all those with whom we come in contact, and beyond.

Buddhism, more than any other religion...except perhaps the religion of science...brings constantly to our attention the profound implications of the fact that we all live in a totally joined up world.

THE END

Nichiren Buddhism in Today's World

The story that brings Nichiren Buddhism into the modern world is a profoundly dramatic one. The extraordinary fact is that it's really only in the past 60 years or so, with the post-war liberalisation and opening up of Japanese society, that Nichiren Buddhism has begun to spread around the world. After his death Nichiren's practice lay locked up in a feudal Japan that was virtually closed off and isolated from the rest of the world. It was sustained by a relatively small population of priests and practitioners who passed it on from generation to generation.

Then, in the turbulent 20th Century, two key events occurred. The first was in the late 20's when a determined and visionary educator named Tsunesaburo Makiguchi, who believed that the only lasting way to achieve genuine social reform in society was through changes in the educational system, found in Shakyamuni's and Nichiren's teachings the powerful philosophical basis he had been seeking, to launch a wholly new approach to education in Japan. He was keenly aware of educational developments in the West, and he wanted to turn Japan away from the impersonal, learning-by-rote regimentation that characterised its educational system, towards an approach that focused much more on each individual student's potential. In 1930 he set up a society with these radical aims, based firmly upon the principles of Nichiren Buddhism. This gradually developed over the following decade into a wider movement of people who both practised and spread the principles of Nichiren Buddhism in Japanese society.

With the rise to power of the military junta in Japan in the 1930's this small but intensely liberal and progressive lay Buddhist organisation, was seen to be something of a threat to the widespread promotion of a nationwide form of worship, Shintoism, dedicated to the support of the Junta's far-reaching military ambitions. Makiguchi, and his closest follower, a man called Josei Toda, were imprisoned because they refused to give up their beliefs. Makiguchi died in prison in 1944, prepared to give up his life, literally for his beliefs. Josei Toda was released in 1945, emaciated and unwell, his health permanently damaged by his ordeal in captivity.

But he had never for a moment given up his practice, and it had clearly created in him an indomitable inner strength. He was released into a totally changed world. Japan had been crushed, many of its cities and much of its infrastructure lay in ruins. Its people were despairing. In 1945 the American General MacArthur, was made supreme ruler in Japan, with powers to oversee the reconstruction of the country and to introduce a raft of liberal measures that were to transform society; measures as radical in that still feudal society as equality for women, freedom of education, and complete freedom of religion.

It was a genuine revolution, not just in the history of modern Japan, but before long, in the global spread of modern Buddhism. From what must have been the lowest point in his own life, and the life of the Japanese people, Josei Toda found within himself the strength and the inspiration to set out once again. He began to speak publicly again about Nichiren Buddhism, with its clearly defined methods of practice for ordinary people, and its powerful message of hope and courage and down-to-earth solutions for the problems of everyday life. To a people who had been crushed by the long years of military dictatorship and overwhelmed by the devastation that fire bombs and nuclear bombs had wrought on their cities, it was a message that served to lift them out of despair. Within the space of just ten years there were many tens of thousands of people who had come to base their lives on the principles of Nichiren Buddhism. And then, within a few years, the hope-filled and intensely practical news that this Buddhism embodied, began to flow out of Japan westwards into Europe, and across the Pacific into the Americas.

Today, the lay Buddhist organisation originally founded by Makiguchi, now called the SGI or Soka Gakkai International (Soka meaning 'value creating' and Gakkai meaning 'society') has spread around the world. It owes much to its crusading leader over the past half century, Daisaku Ikeda, who is one of the most influential and most highly regarded speakers and writers on Buddhism in the world today, and the immense contribution that Buddhist values can bring to today's societies. He has travelled and worked tirelessly to spread the message of Buddhism, both as a solid basis for individual lives, and as a major vehicle for peace and reconciliation in a conflict-ridden world.

The primary quality of the SGI is that it is an enabling organisation. It seeks to bring awareness of what Buddhism is about, and to slice through the many stereotypes that obscure the nature of Buddhist teachings and beliefs, particularly in the western-way-of-life parts of the world. In many ways it acts as a sort of global university, within which, entirely at their own pace and in their own way, peoples of many cultures and widely different backgrounds can study Buddhism and its implications, both for their own lives, and the wider workings of society. To this end the SGI translates and publishes and issues commentaries and observations, and arranges seminars and study course and public debates. It is wholly voluntary in all its activities, you seek it out rather than it seeking you. Through its mediation many tens of thousands of people, from every conceivable background and way of life, and spread across many countries, have chosen to learn how to grow the sense of stability and optimism and well being in their lives, based on the principles of Mahayana Buddhism.

In this sense, the SGI represents in many ways, perhaps the most vibrant modern end of the thread that links us today, directly with the thoughts of the revolutionary teacher who so inspired his audiences with his new vision of individual freedom in Northern India, all those years ago. And religious historians have begun to take note of the scale of the change that would seem to be under way. The late Dr. Bryan Wilson for example, from Oxford, in his work on comparative religion, has written of the way in which it has opened up Nichiren Buddhism as a global, life affirming religion.[1] While Nur Yalman, Professor of Anthropology at Harvard, has gone so far as to describe the social and religious movement inspired by the SGI as a reformation, of similar significance in the history of Buddhism, as the Protestant Reformation has been in the history of Christianity.[2]

So we are talking about a shift to a view of life based on Buddhist principles, which has no precedent, and which is of historical significance.

The Practice

It is important to de-mystify this word practice. The fact is that it is used in very much the same way as one might use it in talking about any other field of human endeavor. The basic objective of any practice is to get better at something. Any sportsman, any musician, any artist knows that unless they train, unless they practice, they cannot possibly attain their full potential. Moreover, having more innate talent doesn't mean less training. The bigger the talent, the more, rather than less those sportsmen and musicians have to train because they have a greater potential to fulfill. Few people train as hard as top class Olympic athletes or concert pianists for example.

By the same token, however inherent the quality of Buddhahood may be, drawing it out into the light of our daily lives requires a real personal commitment to sustained practice. As the famous, world-class golfer Gary Player once said,

"The more I practice the luckier I get!"

In my experience something very similar is true of Buddhism. You will frequently hear Buddhists say that the more they practice the more they feel themselves to be fortunate, or in harmony with themselves and in some way, however difficult it may be to define, in rhythm with the world around them. Unexpected opportunities appear for example, at the most opportune moment, seemingly insoluble problems suddenly unravel, relationships improve, anxieties diminish. That may sound just too good to be true. That doesn't alter the fact however that they continue to occur.

Similarly when Buddhists are aware that they are approaching a time of extra stress or difficulty in their lives, a set of important exams coming up, or stress in a close relationship, or illness or a change of job, they go into training you might say. They deliberately step up their practice, to give themselves the greater resilience and wisdom and self confidence, to be able to see their way through a difficult time, and to help them to drive through the greater turbulence in their environment. It is as deliberate and conscious a process as that. Thus people use the practice as an additional asset available to them. Buddhism is daily life. In many ways that simple sounding phrase is the very heart of the Buddhist message. Trying to learn how to see the problems and the challenges that come ceaselessly, from all directions, as opportunities, opportunities to grow our lives. If you think about it for a moment, that necessarily means developing the *wisdom* to spot them, and the *courage* to grab onto them, because exploiting opportunities inevitably means change, and change takes courage.

In a sense it is rather like the Chinese pictograms that represent the concept of crisis. In fact precisely the same pictograms have two meanings, one meaning is crisis, the other is opportunity. It thus becomes a question of perception. If we perceive the situation as a crisis it threatens to knock us down and steal our hope. If we see the same situation as an opportunity it lifts us up and spurs us on. The situation itself is no different. The only difference lies in our perception, our attitude to the situation.

But that difference makes all the difference, since it empowers us to achieve a radically different outcome. The Buddhist argument essentially is that they are not going to stop coming, those problems. It's a bit like saying something as patently obvious as water is wet. It's not sometimes wet. It's always wet. That is its nature. Just as the nature of life is that it is filled with problems. The only part of the equation over which we have control is our approach to those problems. And the key stage in the process of change is coming to understand that this is not a purely intellectual process. Buddhism suggests that the intellect can only take us so far. We can't simply think our way into a radical new approach to life, we have to work at it, we have to go into training, to acquire that difference of perspective.

That is not an easy truth, either to believe in or to understand. It is not something we are accustomed to doing. If we get a problem the immediate, instinctive, conditioned response is to go to brain. That's what we have always done. That, we believe, is where our powerhouse is.

We are accustomed in the West, highly trained even, to live our lives driven by three primary engines; our intellect and our emotions or how we think and how we feel, and by our persona, or how we look and present ourselves. We place huge store, as indeed we should, on our intellectual ability to think our way through life's problems. We also attach immense value to emotional expression, and perhaps far too much to externals, to physical appearance. Essentially all Buddhism is saying is, hang on a bit, there's more…there is a spiritual resource within that is capable of lifting your total life performance to a new level…your Buddha nature.

Three Basic Elements: Chanting

There are three basic elements to the practice of Nichiren Daishonin's Buddhism. The basic practice is chanting, chanting the phrase Nam Myoho Renge Kyo out loud, rather than repeating a mantra silently within your head. The key point to hang onto is that chanting is clearly a physical action and it has clear physiological effects. For a start it involves moving considerable volumes of air into and out of the lungs for example, and it raises the body temperature. People regularly loosen their tie or take off their jacket when they are chanting. There are many who say that it's very good for the complexion for example, because it powerfully stimulates the circulation and sets the skin tingling.

But above all it is a wonderful and joyful sound, and it is absolutely central to this practice. It is without question the essential driving force, the engine, to initiate and maintain the process of change. Normally it is carried out twice a day. In the morning, to launch you into the day with a wholly positive, up-beat frame of mind. And in the evening basically in the spirit of gratitude for the day that we've had, good, bad or indifferent. If it has been good there is a lot to be grateful for. If it has been bad then you may need to regain the courage and the confidence to tackle the challenges that have arisen. Both morning and evening it is accompanied by the recitation of two brief passages of the Lotus Sutra that express the fundamental Mahayana teachings, on the universality of Buddhahood and the eternity of life.

There is no set time to chant, nor any set period of chanting. As with so many other aspects of Buddhist practice, that is entirely up to the individual. It's your life. You can chant for as little time as you can spare before you have to catch the 8.10 train to work, or to your hearts content, as one of Nichiren's letters puts it. The practice is immensely flexible, shaped to fit in with the demands of a modern life. The key element is the regularity of the practice. Just as we need to refuel our bodies with meals two or three times a day, so Buddhism argues, we need this regular refreshment of our spiritual resources.

What do we think about when we chant? Well the short answer is not a lot. That is not really the point… thinking. The intention if you like is to listen to the rhythm of it, listen to the sound, feel the vibration, enjoy the moment for it's own sake. Give the sound your full attention. The time for thought is before you start, what is it you want to chant about, and after you have finished, when the mind is clear and you are deciding on what action you need to take. What do we chant for? We are chanting essentially to tap into this potential within our lives that helps us to achieve a more positive and optimistic life state. Daisaku Ikeda describes the potential of the practice as limitless, so that is the dominant underlying thought. But you can chant for any goal you wish to achieve, either in the short or long term in your life, and the lives of those around you.

The fact is that people don't often start chanting because they want to save the planet so to speak, or rarely. They are more likely to start chanting for reasons that are much more personal, and closer to their daily life, sometimes outlandish, sometimes selfish. A better house for example, a better job, better health, a happy and successful day. Many people chant for these and other utterly normal worldly desires every day of the week. They are very much part of our ordinary humanity, and the desire for them is real enough. But the common experience is that the very process of chanting Nam myoho renge kyo begins to broaden and deepen our view, and although these initial desires may stay, they begin to be changed and refined and added to. They grow dynamically just as our life grows, having been the initial impetus or the primary cause that drove people towards a greater self knowledge and the desire for greater value creation.

It is in that sense that earthly desires may be said to lead to self enlightenment. Chanting to achieve everyday things in one's life, including material things, runs counter to a widely held misconception about Buddhism, that it is a lot about renunciation, about giving up many worldly things as a necessary step on the road to achieving a higher spiritual condition. That is very much a misconception. Nichiren Buddhism teaches that giving up things, of itself, brings no benefits. It argues that desire is basic to all human life and that as long as there is life there will be the instinctive desire in the hearts of all men and women to make the most of that life; to live, to grow, to love, to have.

Nichiren Daishonin saw with great clarity that little was to be gained from people expending huge amounts of thought and time and energy seeking to extinguish a force that lay right at the core of their lives. On the contrary, he taught, infinitely more is to be achieved, by accepting that wanting things is an essential part of everyone's humanity, and then harnessing it, as a powerful engine for individual development.

Not an intellectual exercise

But let's be clear, we are not talking about a wholly intellectual process. It is in many ways beyond the reach of the intellect alone. There are many stories to be told of people who started chanting in this somewhat inconsequential way, driven purely by personal desires, more often than not without any strong belief in the efficacy of the practice. They now look back and often laugh openly at those somewhat shallow beginnings, in the knowledge of how profoundly their lives and their concerns have been changed.

They continue to chant for their personal desires, but now with a far wider vision if I may put it that way, that extends from their personal on-going human revolution, outwards in ever increasing circles, to take in family and friends and workplace and community and the global society. The ultimate goal of the Nichiren Buddhist is a world made up of people and communities that live in peace one with another. However difficult a goal that may be to achieve, Buddhism reminds us every day with our practice, that it remains a desirable and meaningful objective, so that giving up is not an option. We chant for it and work for it on a daily basis. There is a well known Buddhist text which goes, '*Peace begins with me.*'

Study

The second major element in the practice is study, studying a wide range of things from the letters and other writings of Nichiren Daishonin himself, to commentaries by Buddhist scholars, and accounts by individual Buddhists on the way in which the practice has affected their lives. There is I have to say, a huge abundance of material, because it is such a wide ranging philosophy. That having been said, this is not an *intellectual* practice. The study is not about acquiring knowledge in an essentially egocentric way, as an end in itself. It is about deepening ones understanding of the principles that inform the practice. Nichiren makes no bones about its importance. Indeed he goes so far as to say,

'*Exert yourself in the two ways of practice and study. Without practice and study there is no Buddhism.*'[1]

Taking Action

The third pillar of the practice is taking action, the struggle to fold Buddhist principles and values into the warp and weft of one's daily life, so that they are lived, rather than just perceived or understood. That is a daily struggle. Few things are more difficult to change than ingrained, unconscious patterns of thought and behavior that are often driven by selfishness perhaps, or anger or basic lack of concern for other people's needs. That is part of all our experience. The Buddhist practice drives the inner transformation towards a fundamental respect for one's own life, and respect for the lives of all others. But it is not of course a one way journey, one step forward two steps back is a common experience.

But it is important to emphasize the point that we have touched upon previously, namely that Buddhism is not a morality. That is to say, it does not depend for its moral force on *prescribed* patterns of behaviour. It relies rather on the power of this inner transformation, on people learning how to *accept responsibility* for their own lives and their own actions. This clearly has the potential for far reaching effects not solely on the person at the centre, but on the whole of the society he or she inhabits.

The process begins with the individual. It all begins with the personal determination to change one's own life, but the effect of the changes we make in our thinking and therefore in our behaviour extends way beyond our own life. Indeed, since Buddhism draws no distinction between the individual, and the world around him, the environment in which he lives, the influence spreads out in an ever-widening, never-ending series of ripples.

Since the chanting of the phrase Nam Myoho Renge Kyo is central to this process, what does this phrase mean and where does it come from?

The meaning of Nam-Myoho-Renge-Kyo

Myoho renge kyo is the title of the Lotus Sutra in classical Japanese. It is written in the Chinese pictograms that the

Japanese adopted as their own, in order to create their own written language. The five characters used mean literally *'The Mystic Law of the Lotus Sutra'*

The word Nam, which is placed in front of the invocation is the committal word. It comes from the ancient language of Sanskrit and means among other things, 'to devote ones life to.' So a straightforward literal translation of Nam myoho renge kyo would be *'I devote my life to the Mystic Law of the Lotus Sutra.'* But many volumes have been written to explore the depths of meaning locked up in this simple sounding mantra. That is partly due to the fact that the title given to every sutra is seen in Buddhism to be immensely significant, and is considered to embody the entire teaching that it contains. As Nichiren Daishonin explains by analogy with the name of Japan:

'Included within the two characters representing Japan is all that is within the country's sixty six provinces: the people and animals, the rice paddies and the other fields, those of high and low status, the nobles and the commoners...similarly included within the title, or daimoku, of Nam myoho renge kyo is the entire sutra consisting of all eight volumes, twenty eight chapters, and 69,384 characters without the omission of a single character... the title is to the Sutra as eyes are to the Buddha.'[2]

Moreover, Chinese is an incomparably concise language in which each character can be used to express an immense range of different though related meanings, so that these five characters combine to convey a whole universe of thoughts. But neither of these partial explanations can begin to convey the depth of meaning that Nichiren himself ascribes to this phrase. He describes it as the Universal Law of Life that expresses or embodies within itself the relationship between human life and the entire universe. It embraces he says, nothing less than the *'wisdom of all the Buddhas.'* Shakyamuni expresses something close to that in The Lotus Sutra itself, when he says that this Law, *'can only be understood and shared between Buddhas.'*[3]

That is not in any way referring to some sort of exclusivity. Far from it since the whole purpose of the Lotus Sutra is to convey far and wide, the central concept of the universality of Buddhahood? It is simply saying that words and explanations on their own can only take you so far along the path. You have to practice Buddhism, and experience to some extent its power and potential in your life, before you truly begin to understand it. You have to bite into the strawberry that is, before you can begin to understand what it tastes like.

So I don't think we should be surprised or taken aback, if we find some of these issues elusive and difficult to grasp when we first encounter this practice. They are bound to be. Buddhism is daily life and since life is infinitely complex, Buddhism inevitably will reflect that complexity.

Not a Theoretical Practice

In my own case I have to say I did find it difficult. It was one thing coming to understand the principles that underlie Buddhism, and appreciating just how valuable they could be close to, in terms of human relationships, and further afield perhaps, in terms of how society functions. It was quite another to commit to the practice of chanting a strange mantra, perhaps an hour or more a day. Did I really want to do that? A mantra moreover that carries with it a whole bundle of meanings and associations and implications that are to some extent closed off from everyday experience, and derived from a quite different culture.

That was quite a struggle. If I look back I started chanting for two principle reasons. The people I met who were practising were to be admired in many ways, positive, compassionate, socially responsible, always constructive in their aims and objectives. But above all it seemed to me that there was only one way of coming to understand the true impact of Nichiren Buddhism in my daily life, and that was to allow it into my life.

We are told that you don't have to understand theoretically what this phrase means when you begin chanting, in order to gain the benefits that it will bring. Not at all. The understanding will come as your practice grows. You certainly don't have to hang on to the many layers of meaning locked up in its characters as you chant. It is not an intellectual process in that way. Nor indeed, in my experience, is it a feeling one, in the sense that you shouldn't expect an emotional response. You chant Nam myoho renge kyo in a steady rhythm, as loudly or as quietly as you choose, or as your environment allows, freeing the mind off from any particular concerns, relaxed, listening to the rhythm of the voice, feeling the vibration in the body. The key thing perhaps above all, is to *enjoy* the moment for what it is. If you are thinking about what other more valuable things you could be doing with your time, then it's probably better that you go off and do them.

Nor is it blind faith.

But that having been said, Buddhism clearly teaches that anything resembling blind faith, is not an acceptable basis for practice. Does it work is closer to it? Is it making any difference? Nichiren argues consistently that it is up to us to pose these questions to ourselves all the time. Take nothing on trust, however interesting, however powerful and profound the teaching. Unless it actually enables us to do something better within and with our lives; overcome problems, feel a greater sense of confidence in our own abilities, a greater sense of well being, more compassion and respect for others, more focused on what we are seeking…then what is it for?

As we have seen, in Buddhism the word faith is related not to some external force, but to the strength of our belief in ourselves, firm belief in our inner resources of courage and wisdom and compassion, and our ability to harness them in our daily lives. We may indeed take up the practice initially because we come to value some quality that we see in the Buddhists we meet, or because we are attracted by what they say about the promise embodied in the practice. But in the long run, we can only continue our practice with commitment when we are aware of these kinds of benefits emerging in our own life.

That is certainly true of my own experience. I began slowly, and it was a real struggle for a time, a real struggle. But as I became aware of this profound sense of well being that ran right through my life, I started getting up an hour earlier each morning, wherever I was, at home or on location, so that I could do 45 minutes or so of chanting to launch me into the day.

So let's now look at a fractionally more detailed and yet wholly practical account of the meaning of Nam myoho renge kyo. Not one that carries us off into the deeper realms of Buddhist philosophy perhaps, in case we get lost without trace in such a vast territory, but one that might serve as a working reference, bearing in mind that if it stimulates you to know more you can seek out one of the references in the bibliography.

Nam.

So, the word Nam comes from the Sanskrit word namas and although it is commonly translated as, to devote oneself to, it has a very wide range of meanings. Perhaps the most important among those are the phrases 'to summon up,' or 'awaken,' or 'to draw forth,' or 'to make great effort.' Why is knowing about these different meanings helpful? Because they express subtle differences in our approach or our state of mind when we are chanting at different times. When we are faced with something of a crisis for example we may well be thinking about summoning up, or making great effort, rather than just awakening.

Myoho

Myoho ultimately describes the profound relationship between the very essence of life, or the life force inherent throughout the universe and the literally millions of physical forms in which that life force is manifest or expressed. In Buddhism, everything that exists, sentient and insentient, is both a manifestation of that life force, and subject to the eternal rhythm of life that we have talked about, formation, continuation, decline and disintegration. Everything is subject to that process of change, of impermanence as it is often called. As Nichiren Daishonin defines that thought,

'Myo is the name given to the mystic nature of life, and ho to its manifestations.'[4]

Myoho is made up of two elements, myo, which refers to the unseen or spiritual element that is inherent in all things, and ho, which refers to the tangible, physical manifestation that we can apprehend with our senses. In Buddhism all things, all phenomena have a myo aspect and a ho aspect. They are two different but inseparable aspects of life, 'two but not two,' as Buddhism expresses it, as inextricably interlinked as the two sides of a sheet of paper. You cannot have one without the other.

Thus the ho aspect of a painting for example, is made up of the canvas and the paint that is spread across it. The myo aspect is the feeling or the emotion or the creative energy within the artist as he applied the paint in a particular way, and the emotional impact upon us as we view it. Music similarly has a clearly recognisable ho aspect in the arrangement of the black and white marks or the notes on the page, and the physical vibrations produced by the instruments as they interpret them. The profound myo aspect is the effect the music has on our emotions and feelings, as we receive the sounds produced by the instruments in that particular sequence. As Shakespeare expressed it so pithily in Much Ado About Nothing… it is wholly inexplicable that a sequence of sounds produced on violin strings made out of the guts of a sheep… can move our heart so readily to tears!

If we think of ourselves, ho is used to refer to all the elements in our physical make up that can be observed with the senses, our appearance, the way we stand, the way we walk and talk, the way we gesture with our hands and the various expressions we use to communicate. All the things in fact that enable someone to recognize us as who we are.

But what is quite clear is that so many of those *physical* gestures and movements, the expression in our eyes and the tone and modulation of the voice, the animation in the face, the posture of the body are also an expression of *our inner life,* our myo. The two aspects are, as we have said, inextricably interwoven. As we practice and seek to strengthen the vitality of the myo or spiritual aspect of our lives, there is no question that it has a powerful effect upon our physical persona, the expression on our face, the look in our eyes, our tone of voice, our readiness to smile and so on.

Those are perhaps very obvious examples. Rather more difficult to undertstand, indeed one of the most difficult concepts to accept, particularly if you have a background in science I suspect, is the Buddhist belief that all material existence, everything on earth and in the universe, both animate and inanimate, has a physical and a spiritual aspect. Everything but everything, we are told, has both myo and ho. The tree, the rock, the river, the mountain. A difficult idea undoubtedly, although Buddhism of course, is by no means alone in holding this view. Throughout the length and breadth of human history, artists and poets have been constantly seeking to open our eyes to this truth, in all languages and in all cultures.

Wordsworth for example, when he famously described the dance of a bunch of daffodils,

"The waves beside then danced; but they outdid the sparkling waves in glee:
A poet could not be but gay,
In such a jocund company,
I gazed…and gazed…but little thought
What wealth the show to me had brought:
For oft when on my couch I lie,
In vacant or in pensive mood,
They flash upon my inward eye,
Which is the bliss of solitude,
And then my heart with pleasure fills,
And dances, with the daffodils."

Buddhism stresses this aspect of the continuity and association that runs through all things, so that we are not separate from, but closely linked to everything around us. Thus, in Buddhist terms, statements such as being in harmony with, or being at odds with one's environment may not be simply casual figures of speech, they can represent a fundamental truth; a truth that is the basis for the Buddhist principle of oneness of self and environment. This argues that as we change, gradually strengthening and revealing our Buddha nature through our practice, so that change resonates throughout our environment, sending out beneficial ripples in all directions.

One analogy that paints a graphic, if somewhat simplified picture of the relationship between our myo and ho is that of the horse and cart, or horses and cart to be more accurate.

Our life is the cart, pulled along by our myo horse, or our deepest spiritual energy, and our ho horse, our physical life. In general its true to say that we are accustomed to spending a great deal of time and effort nurturing the strength and well being of our ho horse, because it is so visible and so physically accessible to us. We can look at it in the mirror for example, and worry about its shape. We can feed it three times a day, and take it to the gym to work out, and off to play sports to ensure that it's kept fit and healthy and suitably diverted. As a result we tend very much to equate our happiness or our sense of well being with how well we are getting on with looking after our ho horse.

By contrast we tend to spend relatively little time if any, nurturing and exercising our myo horse, because of course it is wholly unseen and in general has a less powerful presence. The result is imbalance. The wagon of our life is at best pulled strongly off in one direction, the direction governed by our physical needs. At worst it is pulled round and round in circles, repeating patterns of behaviour, because the spiritual side of our make up simply hasn't been nurtured enough to influence, to change that is, our habitual behaviour.

So we can become very much creatures of habit, tending to repeat patterns of behaviour even when they lead to pain and suffering. People very often for example go through a whole series of similar relationships, each one of which might follow a very familiar pattern of rise and fall. What we need to do, Buddhism argues, is to become aware of the danger of imbalance, and to allocate more time and energy to keeping both the ho and the myo horses in a healthy state.

Renge

Renge means lotus flower. It also means cause and effect. The lotus flower, adopted as the title of Shakyamuni's ultimate teaching, is an immensely significant symbol in Buddhism for many reasons. It is a plant with a particularly beautiful flower that grows and flourishes most strongly, in mucky, muddy, swampy environments. In this sense it is taken to symbolise the great potential locked up in every human life, the promise that we can build strong and positive and flourishing lives, however difficult the circumstances and the environment we find ourselves in.

Moreover, the lotus happens to carry both blossoms and seed pods at the same time, simultaneously, and in this sense, it is seen to symbolize one of the fundamental and most important principles of Buddhism, known as the simultaneity of cause and effect. Once again it is a principle with which Buddhism asks us to challenge the way we are accustomed to thinking about our everyday lives and relationships. Basically it argues that every cause we make, good, bad and indifferent, plants a balancing effect in our lives, that will, without fail, sooner or later, make itself felt. Thus there is, for all of us, an on-going chain of causes and effects. That is, if you like, the *fundamental dynamic* of our lives, it ties together the past and the present and the future. Buddhism argues that only by coming to understand this can we grasp fully what it means to take *responsibility* for our actions, and change those inherent tendencies that are causing us to suffer.

So it is a fundamental teaching that has all sorts of ramifications, since we are, of course, making causes all the time, within our own lives and in relation to the lives of those with whom we come in contact, all day every day, in everything we do and say and think. Good causes, good effects; bad causes, bad effects. That process of linked causes and effects is going on all the time. So, in other words, *where* we are now, *who* we are now, *how* we act now, could be seen as the sum of all the causes we have made in the past, that have planted effects in our lives.

At the same time, the causes we are making now contain the seeds of our future. So, that is saying, the key factor in shaping our lives is how we *respond* to the situations that face us now. However much we might feel it to be the case, we are not simply subject to chance and accident that come at us out of our environment. The key factor is how we respond to those situations, the causes that we make, and therefore the effects that we generate. The huge message of hope is that whatever has happened in the past, good positive causes made now, will plant good effects in the future.

Kyo

Just as with myoho and renge, kyo has many meanings, but it is literally translated as 'sutra' or the voice or teaching of the Buddha. It also means, vibration, or sound. So it can be taken to represent the vibrations that spread out from someone in the process of chanting. Indeed there is a common Buddhist saying that '*the voice does the Buddha's work,*' and there is no question that the sound or the vibration that is created by a group of people chanting together, even quite a small group, can be very powerful indeed.

I can still recall with great clarity for example, the very first Buddhist meeting I went to, some time before I actually started practising. It was a dark, cold winter evening, I remember, and we were walking along this street of narrow Victorian houses in West London, with me thinking not particularly positive thoughts, such as '*Oh well, It can't last more than about an hour, this meeting.*' And then as we turned up the short garden path to the house, coming through the closed front door there was this wonderful resonant sound. Strong, confident, vibrant. It actually made the hair tingle on the back of my neck I remember. A sound produced by just a dozen or so ordinary people, chanting Nam myoho renge kyo.

This has been necessarily an all too brief account of the many meanings locked up within Nam-myoho-renge-kyo, meanings that go on being added to and deepened as one's practice goes on. As we've said, it is a continuous journey, a continuous process of discovery.

This practice, focused around the chanting of Nam myoho renge kyo is Nichiren's great legacy to mankind. Nichiren was in many ways a modernist and he makes it clear in his writings that it was fashioned specifically for ordinary people, no matter what place or period they inhabit, 13th Century Japan or 21st century Europe. People with busy everyday lives and much else to grab their attention, to enable them to understand that in the very midst of life's difficulties, it is possible to build lives of hope and optimism and resilience, and yes, great happiness too.

Understanding The Gohonzon

The Gohonzon is a simple rice paper scroll and it marks out Nichiren Buddhism from all other forms of Buddhism. It is you might say its most distinguishing characteristic. Hinayana or Theravada Buddhism, is very much focused on Shakyamuni Buddha, and the worship of him as a unique human being. Mahayana Buddhism by contrast is very much more concerned with the Buddha nature inherent in the lives of ordinary people everywhere, and in Nichiren Buddhism, the Gohonzon, allied to the chanting of the title of the Lotus Sutra, Nam myoho renge kyo, make up the primary means of drawing those qualities of wisdom and courage and compassion out into people's daily lives.

The word 'go' in classical Japanese means 'worthy of honour,' and 'honzon' means 'object of fundamental respect,' so it is clearly an object that is held in the very highest esteem in Nichiren Buddhism. It is also, I have to say, an object of considerable beauty.

The Dai Gohonzon, Dai means 'great' or 'original,' was inscribed by Nichiren on 12th October 1279. The original Gohonzon that he inscribed is still preserved in Japan, at a place not far from Tokyo, but anyone who is prepared to make the personal commitment to practice in accordance with the principles of Nichiren, and to protect and care for their own Gohonzon, receives a smaller block print version to establish in their own house.

This is how members of the SGI practice. It is, I should emphasise, an entirely lay movement, there are no priests. Nichiren himself, during his lifetime, established this pattern of individuals receiving a *personal* Gohonzon, to make it easier for them to practice in a place of their own choosing. Not long afterwards he wrote,

'I Nichiren have inscribed my life in sumi ink, so believe in the Gohonzon with your whole heart'[5]

Sumi is a form of ink used particularly in Japanese calligraphy, and with that immensely simple phrase Nichiren sums up the scale of the task that he had accomplished. He made it abundantly clear to his followers that he regarded it as nothing less than the fulfillment of his life-long mission as a teacher of men.

The characters on the scroll, in Chinese and Sanskrit script, are there to represent the entire reality of human life. Right down the centre, in bigger and bolder characters than the rest and, as it were, illuminating all of the human life they represent, are the characters, Nam-myoho-renge-kyo Nichiren.

That bold central inscription is the key to understanding the nature and the intent of the Gohonzon. When Nichiren wrote, 'I have inscribed my life in sumi.' he is talking about his life as a Buddha, or in the state of Buddhahood. So we have it there in front of us, a representation of what it is that we are seeking to draw out from within our own life, nothing less than our highest life state. It is his great gift if you like, to all of humanity, and in that sense it embodies the fundamental Buddhist principle, first declared in the Lotus Sutra, that all ordinary human beings have the potential for Buddhahood, inherent within their lives.

It is I have to say, difficult to think of an accurate analogy that comes close to expressing what it is that is going on when you chant in front of the Gohonzon. One that comes close is perhaps the musical one. When Beethoven or Mozart for example sat down and wrote out a piece of music, they too were expressing their life state, their passion, their spirit, their elation or melancholy, at that moment in time. An *inner* world translated into bold marks in black ink on white paper. Whatever happens subsequently to that piece of paper, the spirit that flowed through the writer's inner world at that time has been indelibly inscribed on it, *for all of time*.

The sheet of paper with the ink marks might rest unnoticed on a dusty library shelf for decades on end. It might be copied out lovingly by a clerk's hand, or put through a modern digital photocopier to churn out a thousand copies. But whatever journey it travels, when the thousandth copy is placed in front of a musician and played, the *spirit* embodied in the original all those years ago, is, to a greater or lesser extent, brought back to life. So it can fill the room with its sound and its vibration, and recreate in those who hear it, some measure of the spirit that went into it when it was written.

With the Gohonzon, we, in this analogy occupy the role of the musician and we are seeking to recreate the spirit embodied in the original. The Gohonzon depicts all the aspects of our ordinary human life, the good the bad and the ugly, the positive and the negative, the light and the dark. All these aspects of our everyday lives are there, and Nichiren's too, for he was after all an ordinary human being. But they are *illuminated* by the principle that can enable us, however strong our anger or however deep our despair, to move our lives towards the life state of Buddhahood, that Nichiren captured in sumi ink. Nothing is excluded. No life state is rejected. We don't have to *get rid* of anything, or *feel guilty* about anything. The structure of the Gohonzon is there to make clear, that there isn't a life state or a condition that a human being can experience that would in some way prohibit that journey towards our greater self. Everything can be transformed.

That is the huge scale of the promise.

And that really is the Gohonzon's basic purpose, it is something physical to focus on. It is that practical. Something to keep our mind on the task in hand, namely chanting. Nichiren has given us this 'picture' of what it is we are seeking to achieve. It is nothing more than that. Nor, it's important to remember, nothing less.

It is sometimes described as a mirror, that reflects back to us our true nature. Just as we cannot see our face without a mirror to reflect it back to us, so Nichiren argues, we cannot perceive our Buddhahood without the 'mirror' of the Gohonzon to reflect its image.

Does it really happen? Yes. Undoubtedly, and for many thousands of people. Can we clearly say why? I don't believe so. There are many explanations offered but all too often the explanations are couched in terms that are no less mystical than the events in front of the Gohonzon. But then many things in our universe lie beyond the scope of the partial and incomplete vision provided by our intellect.

What the practice in front of the Gohonzon does require is real application and effort, and a commitment to persevere, to give it your best shot. Of course there are ups and downs. You stride forward one month and stand still the next. But the stark reality of course, is that people only continue with this practice because of the benefits that appear in their lives. That has to be the acid test, and the implications are profound. We are not talking about a heaven of whatever form in some hereafter, coming as a reward for the way we live in this life. Buddhism, as we have said so often, *is daily life.* This life, in the here and now. The benefits have to be experienced at home and in the workplace, and in how one feels about life today and tomorrow and the day after.

There is no test more strenuous than real life, and there is no question, the practice of Buddhism continues to pass that test on a daily basis.

List of References

Introduction
The Buddhist Perspective
1. Barack Obama. Commencement Address. June 2009
2. J.F. Kennedy. Commencement Address June 1963

Chapter One
A Question of Our Time
1. Brian Greene. The Elegant Universe
2. Daisaku Ikeda. Learning from the Gosho. The Eternal Teachings of Nichiren Daishonin. P155
3. Richard Dawkins. The God Delusion
4. Dr Richard Sloane. Prof. of Behavioural Medicine Columbia Univ. Feature Time. 23.02.09
5. Noam Chomsky. Language and Problems of Knowledge 1988
6. Prof. Lawrence Krauss. Theoretical Physicist. Article New Scientist. 18.11.06
7. Mary Midgley. Review New Scientist.17.10. 06
8. William Woollard. The Reluctant Buddhist.

Chapter Two
Who Are We?
1. Daniel Goleman. Emotional Intelligence
2. James Shreeve. The Neandertal Enigma
3. Wangeri Maathai. Speaking on BBC Radio 4 documentary. May 2010.
4. Nicholas Humphrey. The Inner Eye
5. Oxford University Neuroscience. Home page.

Chapter Three
What's Religion All About?
1. Daniel Everett. Don't Sleep there are Snakes
2. Prof. Martin Seligman. Article New Scientist. 06.03.10
3. Dr. Andrew Newberg. Director of Research at Center for Integrative Medicine, Thomas Jefferson Hospital and Medical School. Feature Time. 23.02.09
4. Dr. Herbert Benson. Harvard. Timeless Healing: The Power and Biology of Belief
5. Arnold Toynbee Choose Life
6. David Sloan Wilson. Prof. Biological Sciences and Anthropology Briginton University. Article New Scientist. 01.09.07
7. Arnold Toynbee. Choose Life
8. Alex Perry Falling Off The Edge
9. Arnold Toynbee ibid
10. Arnold Toynbee ibid

Chapter Four
What's so Special about Buddhism
1. Edward Conze. Buddhism: A Short History
2. Declaration of Human Rights
3. Richard Causton. The Buddha in Daily Life.
4. The Lotus Sutra Chapter 10

Chapter Six
Buddhism is not a Morality
1. Thich Nhat Hahn. The Heart of the Buddha's Teaching
2. The Mindful Way through Depression. Mark Williams, John Teasdale, Zindel Segal, Jon Kabat-Zinn
3. Edward Conze. Buddhism: A Short History.
4. Roy Baumeister. Florida State University. Journal of Personality and Social Psychology. Vol 74
5. Peter Gollwitzer. New York State Univ. Article in New Scientist 13.09.08
6. Nicholas Christakis. Prof. of Medical Sociology Harvard. Article New Scientist 03.01.09

7. ibid
8. ibid
9. Daisaku Ikeda. Faith Into Action p130

Chapter Ten
A Brief Excursion into the Brain
1. Arnold Toynbee. Choose Life
2. Arnold Toynbee ibid
3. Marcus Raichle. Neuroscientist. Quoted in New Scientist. 08.11.2008
4. Richard Davidson quoted in Richard Layard Happiness p 17 and Time Feature 12.02.2007
5. Jill Bolte Taylor. My Stroke of Insight
6. Jill Bolte Taylor. Ibid.
7. Daniel Goleman. Emotional Intelligence
8. Jill Bolte Taylor. Ibid
9. David Robson. Article in New Scientist 04.09.10

Chapter Eleven
The Mystery of Mind
1. Francis Crick. Quoted feature Time Mag. 12.02.07.
2. Daniel Goleman. Emotional Intelligence
3. Stephen Pinker. Prof. of Psychology Harvard. Feature in Time. 12.02.07
4. Raymond Tallis. The Kingdom of Infinite Space
5. A.C. Grayling. Prof. of Philosophy, Birkbeck College. Article in New Scientist.04.08.10
6. Thich Nhat Hanh. The Heart of the Buddha's Teaching
7. Mark Williams, John Teasdale, Zindel Segal, Jon Kabat-Zinn. The Mindful Way through Depression.

Chapter Twelve
Mind and Body
1. Dr. Dwight Evans, Prof. Of Psychology, Medicine and Neuroscience. Univ. of Pennsylvania. Feature Time. 17.02.03

2. Neal Krause Collegiate Professor of Public Health, University of Michigan
3. Dr Herbert Benson. Timeless Healing: The Power of Biology and Belief

Chapter Thirteen
Changing the Wiring Diagram

1. Alvaro Pascual Leone. Prof. of Neurology. Harvard
2. Daniel Goleman. Emotional Intelligence
3. The Mindful Way through Depression. Mark Williams, John Teasdale, Zindel Segal and Jon Kabat-Zinn
4. Jon Kabat Zin. Univ. of Massachusetts. Director of Center for Mindfulness in Medicine. Cited Richard Layard Happiness p 187
5. Susan Greenfield. Prof. of Pharmacology at Lincoln College Oxford. Speech House of Lords. Feb 2009
6. ibid
7. Article London Evening Standard. 17.03.10
8. Yair Amichai-Hamburger. Director Research Centre for Internet Studies. Article NS 19.12.09
9. Thich Nhat Hanh. The Heart of The Buddha's Teaching

Chapter Fourteen
A Kind of Revolution

1. Professor Martin Seligman. Article Time 07.02.05
2. Sonja Luybomirsky. Psychologist. UCLA Riverside. Article Time 07.02.05
3. Dylan Evans. Emotion. The Science of Sentiment
4. Tal Ben-Shahar. The Pursuit of the Perfect

Chapter Fifteen
The Wealth Delusion

1. Mark Buchanan. Article New Scientist. 21.03.09
2. ibid
3. A.C. Grayling The Greed that will Destroy Us. Article New Scientist 21.03.09
4. Professor Richard Layard Happiness

5. Marc Dreier. Time 25.09.09
6. Prof. Richard Layard. Happiness
7. Gregg Easterbrook. Article Time 07.02.05
8. Andrew Diener. Article Time 07.02. 09
9. Prof. Richard Layard. Ibid.
10. Nichiren Daishonin. Writings of Nichiren Daishonin Vol 1 p3
11. Nichiren Daishonin. Ibid. p851

Chapter Sixteen
A Brave New World
1. Robert Kennedy. Quoted Time article 01.11,09
2. Prof. John Hall. Economist. Article Time 01.11.09
3. Prof Richard Layard. Happiness
4. Daisaku Ikeda World of the Gosho Vol 1.

Appendix A
Nichiren Buddhism in Today's World
1. Professor Nur Yalman. Quoted in Seikyo Shimbun. 26.11.93
2. Bryan Wilson. Human Values in a Changing World

Appendix B
The Practice.
1. Writings of Nichiren Daishonin Vol 1 p 386
2. Ibid p 922
3. Lotus Sutra Chapter 2
4. Writings of Nichiren Daishonin Vol 1 p 4
5. Ibid. p 412